The Real-Time Contact Center

The Real-Time Contact Center

**Strategies, Tactics, and Technologies for Building
a Profitable Service and Sales Operation**

Donna Fluss

AMACOM

American Management Association
New York • Atlanta • Brussels • Chicago • Mexico City • San Francisco
Shanghai • Tokyo • Toronto • Washington, D.C.

This publication is designed to provide accurate and authoritative information in regard to the subject matter covered. It is sold with the understanding that the publisher is not engaged in rendering legal, accounting, or other professional service. If legal advice or other expert assistance is required, the services of a competent professional person should be sought.

Library of Congress Cataloging-in-Publication Data

Fluss, Donna.
    The real-time contact center: strategies, tactics, and technologies for building a profitable service and sales operation / Donna Fluss. — 1st ed.
    p. cm
    Includes bibliographical references and index
    ISBN-10: 0-8144-7256-7
    ISBN-13: 978-0-8144-7256-9
    1. Call centers—Management. 2. Call centers—Computer network resources. 3. Customer services—Management. I. Title.
    HE8788.F58 2005
    658.8'12—dc22

                                                                        2005004120

Printing number

10   9   8   7   6   5   4   3   2

Contents

Preface

After an evolution of 30-plus years, billions of dollars in research and development, and countless implementations, contact centers have reached the advanced stage where they are today. Contact centers have matured from hardware-based systems for delivering customer calls on a first-come, first-served basis, to complex, multichannel, multisite servicing infrastructures. The next 5 years, however, are going to be even more exciting, as real-time contact centers alter the business landscape. Significant technological innovation and changes in strategy and practice are yielding new opportunities to enhance contact centers' productivity, profitability, and contributions to the corporation's bottom line.

Contact centers have evolved from being mere "problem-solving departments," often the home for workers who couldn't do anything else in the company, to being among the most technically sophisticated and complex operating environments in an enterprise. Classically cost-oriented, contact centers have felt the brunt of corporate downsizings and rightsizings and are annually asked to do more with less. Although it's always going to make sense to improve the productivity of any people-intensive function, it's now time to recognize the rightful contribution contact centers make to an organization's bottom line, and to provide them with the resources they need.

Contact centers have complex infrastructures in which multiple systems and managers affect almost every activity and interaction. World-class contact centers strive to optimize the performance of their people, process, and technology in order to deliver an outstanding and differentiated customer experience.

The quality of service matters! Contact centers are the voice of the enterprise to its customers and represent the customers' wants and needs to the corporation—at least when the company is willing to listen. When calling a contact center, customers volunteer all sorts of information about what they want and how they want it. As the focal point of customer communication, contact centers are ideally positioned to generate revenue and contribute significantly to a company's bottom line. Organizations have great opportunity to realize financial benefits from contact centers, but this will require changes in corporate strategy, systems, and policies.

Creating a world-class contact center requires the strong commitment of senior management and innovative departmental leadership. It is essential for contact center managers to have creativity, political savvy, technical know-how, sales and marketing experience, financial skills, and a willingness to collaborate with other departments. Contact center managers must also hone their traditional skills, such as hiring, training, line management, quality management, workforce management, scripting, and selling. And, of course, contact center managers should be willing and able to help customers.

Today, organizations expect overworked and often stressed sales and service agents to be able to listen to customer inquiries and resolve their issues at point of contact more than 80 percent of the time. Increasingly, they are also expected to up-sell, cross-sell, or generate sales leads. Generally, agents must do all of this and still meet stringent productivity goals. But it's unrealistic to expect service and sales representatives to interactively convert phone conversations into revenue unless they are enabled and empowered with the training and technology this requires. Companies cannot afford to waste the tremendously valuable information contained in customer phone conversations, e-mails, web interactions, and self-service sessions.

Between 2005 and 2010, we are going to see contact centers—which today, unfortunately, are still generally cost centers—become a core component of the revenue-generating strategy of most companies. New technology and applications will allow enterprises to understand customer needs, wants, and insights in real time, all at the point of contact. Enterprises will be able to structure the "unstructured" customer communications that currently comprise over 95 percent of contact center interactions and convert them to revenue. Empowered, universal agents will be performing a high value-added job, not merely an entry-level, dead-end position.

The Real-Time Contact Center is a guide to help contact centers reach new and ambitious goals. This book is based on my experience as a contact center strategist who has spent more than 22 years building, managing, merging, analyzing, and consulting with hundreds of inbound and outbound contact centers of varying sizes and sophistication, in a wide variety of industries, including airline, automotive, brokerage, banking, insurance, retail, manufacturing, travel, government, higher education, public safety, energy, health care, and high-tech. I have also consulted with sales and service organization of all types, including service support, field service, collections, security, fraud, help desk, technical support, and employee benefits. The strategies and tactics I present in this book are real and practical, based on hands-on experience and intensive market research.

The key features and benefits of *The Real-Time Contact Center* include:

- Strategic and tactical guidance for converting a reactive, cost-oriented contact center into a real-time, revenue-generating profit center that leverages every customer transaction at point of contact.
- Directions for contact centers to work with sales and marketing departments to increase corporate revenue, profits, customer satisfaction, and loyalty.
- A thorough discussion of organizational, process, and system changes required to structure "unstructured" customer communications, identify insights, and open up contact center information to other internal constituents in near-real time.
- A comprehensive review of contact center technology, process, and implementation resource options. *The Real-Time Contact Center* names leading vendors, gives a framework for choosing among different alternatives, and helps create return on investment (ROI) justification for high-value contact center investments.
- Proven and practical advice on how to successfully manage the continuous business and systems changes required to realize the benefits of the real-time contact center. The book explains step by step how to simultaneously manage the transition of people, process, and technology to a real-time model, while maintaining a high level of service.
- Checklists at the end of each chapter that make it easy to evaluate your company's progress in developing a state-of-the-art contact center environment and determine what steps you need to take.
- A roadmap for successful offshore outsourcing, from the selection criteria through the service level agreement and best practices for managing the relationship.
- Original graphic presentations that clearly illustrate and explain complex industry concepts.

The Real-Time Contact Center is designed for you, the business or technology manager who is dedicated to increasing revenue and customer satisfaction by making the most of every customer interaction. If you are a contact center manager or supervisor who wants to leverage the value and contributions that your department can make to your organization's bottom line, this book is for you. You will find guidance for adapting current strategies and practices, as well as information about existing and emerging technologies and applications that will allow you to capitalize on all revenue opportunities. If you are a sales and marketing manager who wants to partner with your contact center colleagues to realize and exceed your mutual goals, *The Real-Time Contact Center* will show you how. Senior executives will also find invaluable advice on how to leverage the wealth of information in contact centers.

Whether you are managing the contact center or working in another department that needs to strengthen its alignment with the contact center and leverage its capabilities, this book will provide the blueprint you need to accomplish your goals. It will help your company's contact center successfully migrate from a reactive, internally focused, cost-controlling department to a real-time, proactive, engaged contact center where everyone—the enterprise, its customers, and the contact center management and staff—wins.

Thank you for reading my book. I value my readers' comments and questions. You can reach me at realtime@dmgconsult.com. I also invite you to visit our web site at www.dmgconsult.com to learn about innovations in the contact center market.

Acknowledgments

*T*he *Real-Time Contact Center* lays out the strategy for the next generation of contact centers, presented from the perspective of a practi-
tioner turned strategist. It addresses strategy, best practices, technology,
management, people, and process, as all must be in sync for a contact center to be world class, and represents years of study and analysis of all aspects of contact centers—from the most mundane to the most challenging, including how to convert cost centers to profit centers and what
systems and training are required. So many people in thousands of companies have contributed to the development of the strategies presented in
The Real-Time Contact Center. I thank you all.

As I was writing the book, I often called on colleagues and friends to
discuss ideas and concepts. I want to thank the following people for so gra-
ciously sharing their time and allowing me to vet my ideas: Steve Cain,
Vance Christensen, Sarah Fraser, Dave Hardwick, Lisa Hager-Duncan,
Guy Jones, Ed Kawecki, Drew Kraus, David Pennington, Scott Schwartz-
man, Bar Veinstein, and Diane Williams. I ask forgiveness from anyone
whom I inadvertently neglected to include. I also want to thank my edi-
tors, Ellen Kadin, Ellen Schneid Coleman, Gloria Fuzia, and Mike Sivilli
for their great assistance, encouragement, and support.

Finally, I'd like to extend special thanks to four people who could not
have been more generous with their time and assistance: Harold Fluss,
Sam Brown, Karen Eisenberg, and Katrina Rhodes. "Thank you" isn't
sufficient, but it's the best I can do. And yes, dinner is at my house.

The Real-Time Contact Center

1

Transforming Contact Centers into Real-Time Enterprises

Contact centers are real-time organizations. They interact with customers in real time, sell in real time, resolve customer problems in real time, listen to customer needs and wants in real time, identify new sales opportunities in real time, enhance the brand and build customer loyalty in real time, and sometimes, unfortunately, they frustrate and disappoint customers in real time.

Redefining the Contact Center's Mission

Contact centers are generally very good at fulfilling their classical mission: service, sales, or a combination of the two, at the lowest possible cost. For most of the past 30 years, doing a good job at service and sales was enough. But good service alone isn't sufficient anymore; today, enterprises can't afford to ignore the millions of dollars in untapped revenue opportunities that flow through their contact centers in unstructured customer discussions and e-mails. Companies need tools to identify and mine the information hidden in customer communications. The challenge is to capture and analyze the data in these transactions and take appropriate action quickly and effectively so that customers will have a wonderful experience, be completely satisfied, and want to spend more money with your company.

The cost of lost revenue, branding and operational opportunities due to wasted customer information is very high for most companies, but these factors are difficult to measure and organizations often do not make it an organizational priority. Cost containment remains and will continue to be the overriding concern in the majority of contact centers, as 70 to 80 percent of most contact centers' expenses are people related. Focusing on cost containment made sense in the past, when there were few tools for leveraging customer insights at the point of contact and using this information to yield revenue, but innovative and differentiated contact centers are now generating incremental revenue with real-time decision-making tools and best practices.

Contact centers are the focal point of customer interactions with an enterprise. They are practically and strategically positioned to leverage real-time interactions. Customers tell contact center agents when competitors are making better offers and when they are unhappy with corporate policies. Contact center agents know when marketing programs succeed and fail, and they are often the first to know when there is an internal system problem, such as a glitch in billing. This goes far beyond the basics of sales and service—but taking steps to capitalize on this information requires major shifts in organizational mind-set, management, operations, process, and technology. Contact centers that make these changes will accomplish everything they did in the past (including cost containment) and will also give their company a strategic advantage by enhancing each customer's experience and satisfaction and improving the corporate bottom line.

Reactive to Proactive: The Challenge of Transition

For many years, managers have been well aware of missed revenue opportunities in their contact centers, but they were physically separated from senior decision makers, who told them to "just handle customers" and keep their costs down, making it very hard for them to have an impact on the greater corporation. Corporations have often locked contact centers out of the decision-making process and relegated them to second-class status, as compared to sales and marketing functions. Finally, however, contact centers are beginning to participate at the executive level, but having to meet both corporate and departmental objectives poses a variety of challenges.

Contact centers have to transition from being internally focused, reactive departments, concerned mostly with managing costs, to proactive organizations that help to set and influence corporate decisions and goals. It's a difficult challenge, but new contact center performance management applications are helping contact centers find this balance by looking at all aspects of agent and departmental behavior—including productivity, quality, customer satisfaction survey results, sales, and marketing effectiveness—and then tying these measures into enterprise goals. This is a major step in the right direction, albeit one that requires significant changes in procedures, practices, and politics, as well as senior executive support and a great deal of system integration. Finding and implementing effective systems and best practices that help companies increase revenue and decrease costs will drive contact center investment decisions during the next 5 years.

Twelve Top Trends in Contact Centers

If the economy continues to grow, the next 5 years are going to be very exciting for contact centers. While slow to change, the contact center market now offers a great deal of innovation and many new opportunities for end-user companies. As enterprise customers start to buy new and open solutions, the pace of innovation will certainly pick up speed. The top trends in the contact center market are the following (see Figure 1.1):

1. *Internet Protocol (IP)*. Internet protocol, which deals with voice and data transactions and facilitates multisite activities, is here to stay, even though companies have not rushed out to invest in new IP contact centers. Enterprises interested in replacing their contact center solutions should seriously consider an IP contact center if they are "greenfield" (without an existing contact center), relatively small in size, and this investment doesn't require a wholesale replacement of their existing voice and data infrastructure. Larger organizations looking to invest should not wait. Instead, they should buy open, hybrid platforms that include both time division multiplexing (TDM) and IP capabilities that they can fully convert to an IP contact center in the future without a total system replacement.
2. *Voice and Data Convergence*. Most companies are converging their voice and data networks. However, this often results in turf battles over who owns the transactions, with the data side usually winning. It's time to put internal political battles aside and move forward to realize the technical and organizational benefits.
3. *Hardware-Independent Systems*. Customers want the flexibility to make software decisions that are not tied to specific hardware platforms and are increasingly demanding hardware-independent solutions.

Figure 1.1: Contact Center Trends

Contact Center Trends

1. Internet protocol (IP)

2. Voice and data convergence

3. Hardware-independent systems

4. Integrated multi-vendor solutions

5. Simplified operating environments

6. Platform extension

7. Organizational access to contact center transactions and data

8. Return on investment (ROI) and total cost of ownership (TCO) calculations

9. Hosting/on-demand services

10. Offshore outsourcing

11. Targeting small and mid-size businesses (SMBs)

12. Migration from cost centers to profit centers

Source: DMG Consulting LLC.

Instituting flexible systems is an important step on the critical path to opening enterprise systems and sharing contact center data on a timely basis.

4. *Integrated Multivendor Solutions.* End users want to have free choice in selecting systems and applications without being hampered by the tech-

nical limitations of their contact center infrastructure providers. They want systems and applications that are open, flexible, and easy to integrate. The good news is that many of the contact center infrastructure and platform providers are now delivering systems that can integrate with multivendor solutions.

5. *Simplified Operating Environments.* End users are demanding openness and flexibility, but they are also striving to simplify their operating environment and make it easier to manage.

6. *Platform Extension.* Contact center vendors are expanding their footprint to include systems and applications—such as interactive voice response (IVR), outbound, and logging—that were previously purchased separately and then integrated.

7. *Organizational Access to Contact Center Transactions and Data.* Sales, marketing, operations, finance, and the executive suite are increasingly interested in understanding customer behavior, needs, wants, insights, and concerns. There is a great demand for solutions that structure the content of customer conversations and make this information available to other parts of the organization for analysis and action.

8. *Return on Investment (ROI) and Total Cost of Ownership (TCO) Calculations.* Organizations use ROI to help decide between two or more technology options, while TCO is a measure that facilitates management of assets on an ongoing basis. These are complementary financial measures intended to help organizations realize the greatest benefit at the lowest cost. It's no longer sufficient to have the lowest acquisition cost. End users are now appropriately looking at the ongoing operational and support costs of investments. Companies must seriously address concerns such as initial purchase price, ongoing costs, ease of use and integration, and scalability.

9. *Hosting/On-Demand Services.* The hosting offerings available today are very strong functionally and are viable alternatives to a long-term investment. Hosting, also known as on demand, is attracting the attention of contact center management. It's an effective way of acquiring new platforms, solutions, or applications without a large commitment of time or resources.

10. *Offshore Outsourcing.* As cost control remains the top issue in most contact centers, offshore outsourcing, which can reduce people-related expenses by 50 to 60 percent, is an option that demands serious consid-

eration. However, the savings are decreasing, and offshore sites, particularly in India, are now confronting some of the same challenges as United States–based sites: high agent turnover, ongoing training, and quality concerns.

11. *Targeting Small and Mid-Size Businesses (SMBs).* There are more SMBs around the world than large enterprises. Small and mid-size businesses are hungry for effective and feature-rich applications that are priced appropriately for them. Vendors are realizing the potential of SMBs and have started to deliver solutions for this market. Much work remains to be done to satisfy SMBs, but the market potential is huge both in the United States and abroad.

12. *Migration from Cost Centers to Profit Centers.* For most of the 1990s, the industry talked about transitioning contact centers from service departments (cost centers) to organizations that also sell and generate profits. It has taken a long while, but an increasing percentage of contact centers now service and sell.

Each of these trends represents opportunity and innovation for contact centers. Internet protocol, for example, greatly simplifies multisite challenges and facilitates offshore outsourcing. Voice and data convergence allows companies to create simplified operating environments, but only if they properly manage the transition.

Seizing Opportunities for Growth

Few, if any, contact centers will address and take advantage of all of these trends. It is generally a better idea to concentrate on one or two areas at a time instead of attempting to fix everything at once. It is essential to be aware of and understand industry developments and to note the general direction of the market in order to take advantage of the opportunities that will yield the greatest benefits for a particular company, its customers, and its partners.

Contact Center Maturity Checklist

The following checklist will help you determine if your contact center is prepared to shift from a closed, reactive, and proprietary environment to one that freely and easily shares customer information in near-real time with stakeholders, senior decision makers, and the executive suite.

Yes No

❑ ❑ Do your sales, marketing, and service (contact center) departments meet regularly to discuss customer-facing programs and issues?

❑ ❑ Do all of your customer-facing departments share common goals and standards for success?

❑ ❑ Does your contact center management actively participate in setting corporate goals?

❑ ❑ Does your contact center have sales and revenue goals?

❑ ❑ Do you have a mechanism (processes and systems), such as performance management, for measuring how well the contact center delivers on its internal/departmental and external/corporate goals?

❑ ❑ Do the standards used to measure agent performance reflect productivity, quality, contribution to sales and revenue, and customer satisfaction?

❑ ❑ Do you have a formal report or scorecard that reflects all agent activities in one document?

❑ ❑ Do agents receive weekly or monthly performance reports?

❑ ❑ Are agents rewarded for achieving sales goals, even if they have increased their average talk time?

❑ ❑ Have you invested in applications, such as speech analytics or contact center real-time analytics, that capture, analyze, and synthesize the data in unstructured customer conversations and communications?

If you answered No to more than half of these questions, then your contact center is lagging behind and losing ground to competitors. It's time to assess your operating environment and strategy and begin the transition to a real-time contact center that's as dedicated to the overall customer experience as it is to leveraging every single customer contact to improve your company's bottom line.

2

The Development of the Real-Time Contact Center

According to Gartner Inc., a leading information technology consulting company, a contact center is a multichannel and multipurpose (sales, marketing, and customer service) organization that serves a variety of constituents (customers, prospects, investors, and partners) in a logically consolidated but physically disaggregated setting. What differentiates a contact center from a call center is that the latter handles phone calls (answered by either agents or an interactive voice response [IVR] system) only, while the former involves all types of customer transactions including phone calls, e-mails, chat sessions, and web collaborations. Call centers were sufficient for satisfying customer needs until 1996, when the Internet began to alter the technical landscape and consumers began using e-mail to communicate with companies. Companies that want to satisfy their customers must now allow them to communicate in their channel of choice and provide the same consistently high level of service in all channels—a daunting challenge for most enterprises.

What Is a Real-Time Contact Center?

Practically speaking, all contact centers that handle live inquiries from customers, partners, investors, or prospects are real-time organizations and always have been. However, a real-time contact center is designed to take advantage of every customer-initiated transaction in real time or near-real time, either when the customer is on the line or immediately thereafter, within time frames established by the customer, to ensure a great experience and complete satisfaction. It's a service and sales environment where, after the initial customer inquiry or sales request has been addressed, the agent or self-service system uses the information provided by the customer, in real time, to extend the relationship. This means that the contact center must hire and train agents who are as comfortable with selling as they are at servicing. It must have real-time systems that are able to spot and assess a customer opportunity while the customer is still on the line and supply the agent with one or more new revenue, retention, or loyalty-enhancing opportunities to present to the customer. The contact center must also be able to capture, track, analyze, and take action on competitive, operational, and policy issues identified during the customer interaction. Further, the contact center must have a method for sharing relevant aspects of this transaction with sales, marketing, operations, the executive suite, and the corporate data warehouse so that the results can be analyzed and acted upon.

How the Real-Time Contact Center Impacts the Corporation

Contact centers have always been real-time organizations. The difference now is that companies around the world recognize the significance and benefit of doing business in real time. Real-time transactions have the potential to reduce expenses, time delays, and redundant activities while increasing profits and enhancing customer satisfaction and loyalty. Since contact centers are already doing business in real time, unlike many other business units that would require retooling to do so, they are positioned to deliver some of these benefits immediately. Nevertheless, contact centers need new processes, staff, training, and systems to be positioned to optimize each and every customer contact.

From Call Router to Service Provider: The Expanding Role of the Real-Time Contact Center

Contact centers have matured rapidly, moving from primitive hardware-based call routers to sophisticated software-driven solution providers that add value to every customer transaction. Changes in process and people have accompanied each stage of the contact center's technological development.

Missed Calls: Automatic Call Distributor to the Rescue

The first contact center, called an automatic call distributor (ACD), was delivered in the mid-1970s to help the airline industry answer sales calls on a first-come, first-served basis. Airlines realized that every missed call represented lost sales and that the cost of the technology could quickly be offset by increased revenue. Early ACDs applied queuing theory to incoming phone calls and established an efficient method of managing customer inquiries. While the first ACDs were built for a sales function, it quickly became obvious that an ACD system could also be used to efficiently and cost-effectively manage the ever-increasing volume of customer service transactions. (See Figure 2.1.)

Operational Efficiency: The Phone Center Stage

By the mid-1980s, industry best practices had been put in place and new management applications, such as workforce management, were available to further improve the efficiency of increasingly sophisticated service and sales organizations. New vendors entered the ACD market and the phone center was introduced. A phone center differed from the classic ACD environment in several ways:

1. Its physical hardware footprint was significantly smaller.
2. It used software for processing and to reduce hardware requirements.
3. It was designed to be managed by end users instead of by the telecommunications group.
4. Its software orientation allowed for the introduction of complementary technology to further enhance operational efficiency, including computer telephony integration (CTI) and IVRs. Touch-tone IVRs were introduced to automate the handling of inquiries and keep them from escalating to expensive phone center agents. Computer telephony integration, in turn, was developed to automatically deliver the customer's account information to the agent's desktop at the same time as the call, so that an agent wouldn't have to spend time keying in the customer's account number, an activity that typically takes between 8 and 15 seconds.

Figure 2.1: Contact Centers: A Brief History

Contact Centers: A Brief History						
Phase	PBX	ACD	Phone Center	Call Center	Contact Center	Real-Time Contact Center
Technology	PBX, key systems, central office–based.	ACD, routing calls, work force management.	Conditional call routing, IVR, CTI, call logging, reporting.	"CRM suite" desktop, integration of front and back office systems, skill-based routing, call blending, speech recognition, QA.	Universal queue, IP, ERMS, chat, reporting, CEM.	Multichannel communications platform. Real-time analytics, text categorization of unstructured data, performance management, web services.
Strategy	Make customers go away.	Answer calls on first-come, first-served basis. Efficiency and cost containment.	Efficiently, productively and politely handle calls. Use IVR to automate calls. Increase first call resolution.	CRM Integrate front and back office systems to improve customer satisfaction and provide differentiated, cost-effective service.	Displace calls with web-based self-service technology. Use contact center to increase revenue.	Open contact center and customer data to enterprise decision makers. Integration of sales, marketing, and service activities. Convergence.
Management Issues	Lack of automation and standards for efficient customer service.	Need to develop and establish service culture, expertise, and best practices.	Balance enterprise needs for productivity with customer satisfaction.	Leveraging people, process, and technology to reduce calls to live agents.	Transition call center to multi-purpose/multi-channel support organization that is logically consolidated but physically dispersed. Multiskilled, flexible, and cost-effective agents.	Build processes and systems to capture, analyze, and use near-real-time data. Optimize contact center interactions. Engage customers.

Source: DMG Consulting LLC.

Increased Productivity: The Call Center

At the end of 1980s, the "phone center" name had given way to "call center," and with the change in terminology came further technological advancements and best practices. Leveraging people, process, and technology became essential, as it was understood that people-related expenses account for 70 to 80 percent of a call center's total costs. The mantra of the call center became "do more with less," as these organizations struggled to contain the growing expenses associated with unprecedented increases in call volumes.

Enterprises invested in new applications, best practices, and training to improve the effectiveness of their call centers. New technologies were introduced, including customer relationship management (CRM) suites that integrated front and back office systems to improve the efficiency of call handling, and quality assurance (QA) to review how well agents adhere to internal policies and procedures.

Although presented as products to improve quality, QA tools were generally used to increase efficiency. Other innovations included skill-based routing to direct calls to the most qualified representative; call blending to make more efficient use of inbound/outbound sales and service agents; scripting to improve the delivery of sales and service pitches; and speech recognition to improve the efficiency of the IVR. While all of these applications improved quality, they were adopted because of their ability to increase productivity, either by reducing average talk time with better automation or by eliminating the need to speak to an expensive live agent.

Flexibility and Integration: Contact Centers and Customer Relationship Management

The CRM era began in the early to mid-1990s, between the call center and contact center phases. With it came CRM suites, another set of call center automation tools intended to improve the efficiency of call center agents. By 1998, CRM suites had taken on a life of their own and were considered the most important technology within the call center. For the first time in its short history, the ACD was no longer viewed as the primary infrastructure component of the service and sales call centers, but instead was being forced to make changes in order to integrate with CRM suites. (In the past, the call center vendors had dictated all of the integration requirements.)

While this phase lasted only 2 years (1998 to 2000), the impact was significant and lasting. Previously proprietary and often inflexible call center solutions and vendors were finally being forced to open up their systems and begin the migration to more standards-based and easily integratable platforms, the first step on the critical path to sharing call center activities, resources, and data with the rest of the enterprise.

New Channels for Service and Support: Rise of the Internet and E-Business

The Internet and e-business became hot in 1996–1997, at the same time as CRM, and were accompanied by new communication channels that drove the development of web-based customer service and self-service. It took a couple of years, but by 1998, companies realized that basic service and support needs were the same regardless of the channel. Contact centers (also known as *interaction centers*) were formed to address e-mail and chat inquiries in addition to phone calls.

The shift to contact centers that began in 1997 involved much more than a name change. As in the other phases, new technology was developed to make the service and support organization more productive. However, this time, the introduction of new channels forced a complete business process redesign and an overhaul of service and support organizations, including the ACD.

Although contact center infrastructure had shifted to a software orientation in the 1980s, the platforms were still hardware-based and could not easily be adapted to seamlessly incorporate the new internet-based, data-oriented channels. A goal of the contact center environment is to handle all channels equally—applying the same business rules and work flow and providing standardized reporting regardless of the channel through which transactions are processed. It was very difficult for most of the leading contact center vendors (also known as switch manufacturers) to deliver new technology to accomplish this goal. The demand for standardized service delivery thus forced a change in technology platforms and began the true shift to software-driven solutions.

Technological Innovation: Emergence of Internet Protocol Technology

By the mid-1990s, Internet protocol (IP) technology was capturing the attention of the marketplace. Internet protocol was introduced in the 1970s and standardized in 1981. By the late 1990s IP was being heralded as a more efficient method for moving calls and provided a technical foundation for a new generation of switches. Internet protocol switches were viewed as having the potential to replace the original time division multiplexer (TDM)–based switches. Internet protocol has the advantage of not differentiating processing based on the type of transaction, whether voice or data. It is also a more efficient and cost-effective method of handling transactions among multiple sites, an important requirement for complex contact center environments.

It took until 2003 for IP to be accepted as a viable technology. Mainstream adoption of IP-based contact centers is expected to begin in 2005. As of the end of 2004, few contact centers are replacing their entire TDM-based systems with new IP-based solutions. However, end users are now hedging their investments by purchasing new switches that can handle both TDM- and IP-based processing, laying the foundation for a future cut over to IP.

Very significantly, to meet the needs of contact center and IP users, switch manufacturers have been forced to deliver new platforms that are more open and nonproprietary, although there is still much room for improvement in the continued migration to real standards-based processing.

Maximizing the Value of Each Contact: The Advent of Real-Time Contact Centers

Real-time contact centers are just beginning to come of age and represent another major shift in the market. The basic concept behind the real-time contact center is that it's an open environment (technically and physically) that facilitates sharing of customer information and opportunities with the rest of the enterprise on a timely basis. What this means practically is that there is going to be a shift away from managing transactions (calls, e-mails, chat sessions)—the historical emphasis of contact centers—to maximizing the value of each interaction. Building this type of organization will require significant enhancements to what is already a complex systems and operational infrastructure.

The real-time contact center has to be able to do everything it did in the past, but now it must have an infrastructure that is open and standards-based, facilitating information sharing between all enterprise constituents interested in customer behavior—sales, marketing, operations, research and development (R&D), finance, and the executive suite. Delivering a truly open contact center platform that can be integrated with existing enterprise applications (enterprise resource planning [ERP] or supply chain systems) is a massive task, and the vast majority of enterprises—more than

95 percent of end-user companies—are just beginning to address it. While doing the integration is challenging, the technologies to do the job exist and work.

The more difficult challenge for enterprises is figuring out how to capture and structure the customer communications flowing through contact centers so that they can be mined for customer insights, intents, opportunities, and needs. Speech analytics and text-categorization technologies required to do the job are at least 3 to 5 years from maturity, although these solutions are already making contributions in leading-edge enterprises. In the meantime, enterprises can't afford to waste the highly valuable content included in customer interactions and are going to have to develop best practices to complement these existing but relatively immature technologies. Organizations that achieve this goal cost-effectively differentiate themselves and have a strategic advantage over those that continue with the original mission of contact centers—providing outstanding sales and service support—critical goals but increasingly only one component of the contact center mission.

Achieving Outstanding Service: Optimizing People, Process, and Technology

One person can provide outstanding customer service and sales support to a small group of customers without technology—paper, pencils, and Post-it® notes will do the job. But if a company wants to provide consistently outstanding service to a large group of customers, it must have a sophisticated servicing infrastructure that is fully integrated with its sales, marketing, and electronic commerce systems. Ideally, the servicing system should also be integrated with the ERP and supply-chain systems environments so that agents will have a complete view of each customer's relationship with the enterprise.

Contact centers are more than just the sum of their technology. The greatest technology cannot replace the impact of well-trained service representatives or salespeople, but it can surely improve their productivity, quality, and performance. And, while technology can automate and help standardize and institutionalize best practices, it can't create them. The best contact centers leverage people, process, and technology and constantly review their operating environments in search of new ideas and processes to improve performance.

Figure 2.2: Contact Center Cost Structure

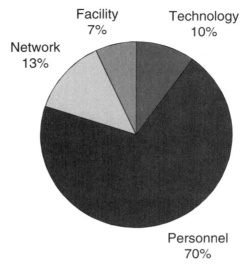

Facility
7%

Technology
10%

Network
13%

Personnel
70%

Sources: Gartner Dataquest and other contact center benchmark studies.

Contact Center Cost Structure

Building a contact center for a medium to large-size enterprise today costs $1 million to $50 million just for systems and implementation, according to Gartner, Inc. Once the initial installation is done, equipment costs will comprise approximately 10 percent of ongoing expenses, the facility (rent and occupancy) 7 percent, and network charges 13 percent.

The overwhelming majority of ongoing costs are people related. (See Figure 2.2.) These expenses include hiring, training, salary, benefits, and attrition. While the numbers vary based on technological complexity, purpose, and size, the cost breakdown will be relatively similar for all United States–based contact centers. (Note that outsourced contact centers in places like India and the Philippines shift the cost structure and decrease agent-related expenses.)

As can be seen in Figure 2.2, people-related expenses account for 70 to 80 percent of the cost of a contact center. The number will lean toward 70 percent for a contact center handling mostly high-volume/low-touch transactions, like a bank, where the primary customer issue remains "What's my balance?" The 80 percent figure applies mostly to low-volume/high-touch contact centers, like help desks, where the typical inquiry lasts 8 to 15 minutes.

Contact Center Performance Management

Contact center performance management is a relatively new entrant in the contact center market. It is a method of measuring contact center adherence to internal and external performance standards. It uses a combination of best practices, tools, and applications intended to create scorecards and real-time dashboards to help align contact center key performance indicators (KPIs) and metrics with corporate goals. This transforms the contact center into an active contributor to the enterprise's profitability. (See Figure 2.3.) Contact center performance management is expected to be adopted by mainstream users during the next 3 years and should be a commonly accepted contact center practice by 2006.

Optimizing the Performance of Contact Center Agents

Because people related expenses account for such a large percentage of the overall cost structure, maximizing agent productivity is appropriately the highest priority in the majority of contact centers. However, it's a mistake when productivity becomes the only goal. While it's important to optimize the performance of contact center agents, it's critical to find a balance between productivity, performance, quality, and customer satisfaction. Contact centers that reward only productivity will find that quality and performance suffer, resulting in customer dissatisfaction and ultimately attrition. Therefore, it's essential for contact centers to find the right mix of the following components:

- *Productivity* (calls per hour, average talk time, e-mails per hour)
- *Performance* (save rates, closed sales)
- *Quality* (agent adherence to policies and procedures)
- *Customer Satisfaction*

Added Value of the Real-Time Contact Center to Sales and Marketing

Unfortunately, in most organizations, the service, sales, and marketing groups do not have great appreciation or respect for one another. Too often, marketing creates new programs in a vacuum without inviting input from

Figure 2.3: Contact Center Key Performance Indicators

Contact Center Key Performance Indicators		
Productivity	**Quality**	**Performance**
Calls handled/hour	Quality evaluation scores	Customer save rates
E-mails handled/hour	% of complaint calls	Sales rates
Chat sessions handled/hour	Customer survey results	Number of new leads collected and passed to sales
Average talk time	Adherence to policies and procedures	Number of up-sells/cross-sells
Average wrap time	E-learning test scores	Number of new customers acquired
Average work time	Customer stress level analysis	Identification of operational issues
First-contact resolution rate	Appropriate use of wrap-up system	Identification of competitive challenges
% of calls fully handled by IVR		
% of inquires resolved on web site		
Agent schedule adherence		
% of time agents are available		
Average speed of answer (ASA)		
% of calls answered within X seconds		
% of calls abandoned		

Source: DMG Consulting LLC.

the service department. The sales department often initiates a new campaign without notifying the contact center, which learns of the campaign only when customer complaint calls begin. The ideal situation would be for all customer-facing organizations to share the same corporate goals and for all three departments to share the responsibility for each other's failures and successes. Contact center performance management is a new structure that, if supported by senior management, may very well help to achieve this goal.

There are very practical reasons why sales and marketing organizations are finally reaching out to their contact center counterparts. Response rates from sales and marketing campaigns have been decreasing at an alarming rate. While there are always exceptions to the rule, response to an outbound campaign (even before the Do Not Call [DNC] legislation of 2003) is typically a dismal 1 to 3 percent. If this weren't bad enough, it sounds even worse when the numbers are turned around: 97 to 99 percent of the sales and marketing dollars invested in most campaigns are being wasted. Poor performance is a great attention-getter, and this is what it took to motivate sales and marketing organizations to ask their contact centers for help in improving response and closure rates.

The information required to enhance the results of marketing campaigns and sales programs passes through contact centers daily. The challenge is to capture, structure, understand, and leverage this information for the benefit of the corporation *and* to do so before it's too late. A real-time contact center is designed to use customer information at the point of contact to realize the greatest return from each transaction while providing an outstanding experience to each customer.

Real-Time Contact Center Evaluation Checklist

Establishing a real-time contact center will differentiate you from your competitors. It positions your service infrastructure to offer proactive and engaging service that enhances your company's overall profitability and brand. The following checklist will help you determine your company's readiness for building a real-time contact center.

Yes No

❏ ❏ Is your company leveraging its inbound customer interactions to increase sales?

❏ ❏ Does your company have systems to capture and identify new revenue and customer retention opportunities hidden in customer transactions?

❏ ❏ Does your contact center have a formal process for capturing and sharing customer insights and competitive information with sales, marketing, product development, operations, and senior management on a timely basis?

❏ ❏ Are your contact center customer service agents effective at up-sell/cross-sell?

❏ ❏ Have the success rates of your outbound sales campaigns improved during the past two years?

❏ ❏ Have you developed new marketing strategies to minimize the impact of DNC legislation on your campaign response rates?

(continues)

☐ ☐ Do your sales, marketing, and customer service groups share common goals?

☐ ☐ Is your contact center respected by sales and marketing?

☐ ☐ Is your annual contact center agent attrition rate below 10 percent?

☐ ☐ Have your investments in contact center infrastructure and CRM initiatives realized the projected returns?

If you answered No to more than half of these questions, then you are well positioned to begin the migration to a real-time contact center that will streamline your operating environment, improve the performance of the call center, enhance customer satisfaction, and increase revenue and profitability.

3

Contact Center Infrastructure

eal-time contact centers are technically sophisticated operating environments that use anywhere from 1 to more than 46 systems or applications to process transactions (calls, e-mails, web chats, faxes, etc.). Transactions can be processed by multiple systems, some that are premise-based, some hosted (sometimes referred to as "in the cloud"), and some that are outsourced.

In 2003, there were 60,026 contact center systems and 5,717,361 agent shipments (agent positions) in North America, according to Gartner. DMG Consulting LLC estimates that 65 percent of contact center systems and 70 percent of agent positions are located in North America. The estimated number of worldwide contact center systems and agent positions are 92,348 and 8,167,659, respectively. The breakdown of contact center systems and agent positions in North America for small (1 to 20 seats), medium (21 to 75 seats), large (76 to 400 seats), and very large (more than 400 seats) contact centers is shown in Figure 3.1.

Keep in mind that these figures include both formal and informal contact centers. Studies have shown that as many as 20 to 30 percent of employees in a typical financial services company may be involved in contact center activities, even though their job function may not be labeled that way. An informal contact center may use a simple handset programmed in a "hunt" fashion to search for an available person in a predefined group, such as account administrators or secretaries. At the other extreme, a sophisticated, formal contact center will use a multimillion-dollar ACD to process incoming calls and match service levels based on customer value.

Figure 3.1: Contact Center and Agent Positions in North America

Size	North America System Count	North America Agent Positions
Small		
1–20 Agents	29,511	389,836
Mid-Size		
21–75 Agents	20,046	1,053,371
Large		
76–400 Agents	8,661	2,221,271
Very Large		
401-plus Agents	1,808	2,052,883
Total	60,026	5,717,361

Source: Gartner Dataquest Market Statistics "Market Forecast: Call Centers, North America, 1998–2008," Dew Kraus, September 2004.

The Changing Business Landscape Alters the Contact Center's Mission

Recent innovations in corporate thinking have altered the business landscape and changed the charter of contact centers from reactive service providers and order takers to proactive, engaged customer advocates and sales forces. Companies that engage their customers have a competitive advantage in an era when service is often the only differentiator between otherwise indistinguishable products. Engaged businesses anticipate and proactively address the needs of their customers in real time. Delivering real-time service builds lasting and profitable relationships, making businesses more productive and reducing expenses by optimizing the use of resources to satisfy each and every customer.

Using your contact center to proactively engage customers will require changes throughout the corporation, from the executive suite to contact center agents. Senior decision makers must invite contact center managers to participate in corporate goal setting, and the contact center must be given objectives that go beyond service, including revenue, loyalty, branding, and the building of lasting relationships. But contact centers can never lose sight of cost containment, as they remain one of the most expensive, people-intensive departments within companies. Maximizing the return from every real-time customer interaction requires standards-based, open, and integratable systems that facilitate information and data sharing both to and from the contact center.

Many of the installed contact center systems are closed and proprietary.

In the past, it didn't really matter, as contact centers were often geographically, organizationally, and practically separated from corporate product management, revenue, and profitability goals. But no longer. Real-time contact centers are engaging customers on all fronts and need open, flexible systems to deliver cost-effective and differentiated service.

Essential Components of Contact Center Infrastructure

To keep a contact center operating, core infrastructure components are essential, including: ACD, IVR, speech recognition, CTI, network management, dialer, and universal queue (UQ). As seen in Figure 3.2, the systems and applications can be segmented by function.

The Heart of the Center: Automatic Call Distributor

If there is only one system in a contact center (and there are many that have just one), it is an automatic call distributor (ACD). Automatic call distributors are real-time systems designed to efficiently process—receive, queue, route, and assign—large volumes of incoming calls to ensure that they are handled on a timely basis. At their most basic, ACDs deliver calls on a first-come, first-served basis to the "most available" agent (the one waiting the longest). System enhancements allow ACDs to assign calls based on routing rules defined by the organization. Automatic call distributors, the heart of the contact center infrastructure, are used for many purposes, including customer service, technical support, internal and external help desk, sales, collections, fraud prevention, security, consumer affairs, employee benefits, government services, and education services.

Self-Service: Interactive Voice Response

After the ACD, the interactive voice response (IVR) is generally the second most essential system in a contact center. IVR is a form of call processing self-service. These systems are critical because they typically displace 30 to 85 percent of calls that would otherwise require the assistance of a live agent. Interactive voice response systems are programmed to respond to dual-tone multifrequency signaling (DTMF, or touch-tone) inputs from the telephone. During an IVR experience, customers can select

Figure 3.2: Contact Center Architecture

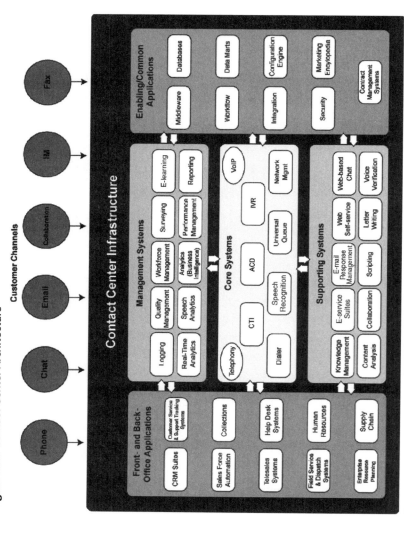

Source: DMG Consulting LLC.

information and assistance from a self-service system. The IVR is menu-driven and prompts customers with questions. Customers respond by pressing keys on their telephone keypad.

Self-Service: Speech Recognition

During the past three years, speech recognition applications have become more common in contact centers. The adoption of speech recognition solutions is expected to be greater in 2005 than in any prior period, as the technology is mature and the use of standards is making these systems easier to deploy. Speech recognition applications are similar to IVRs in that they automate calls that would otherwise be handled by agents but are unlike touch-tone IVRs in that users communicate with these applications by speaking. As of 2004, speech recognition systems are slowly starting to supersede touch-tone IVR applications, as they are easier for customers to use.

Computer Telephony Integration

Computer telephony integration (CTI) is an application that uses data provided from a call, such as the customer's phone number, to access account information or other relevant data. The most basic and common use of CTI is screen pop or "sync," which presents the customer's account information to an agent at the same time as the call is delivered. Like IVR and speech recognition, CTI improves agent productivity. In the case of CTI, it does so by eliminating the time agents spend requesting, inputting, and retrieving each customer's account information. Similarly, CTI improves the customer experience by minimizing delays and time wasted on data retrieval. CTI is increasingly used in real-time contact centers to identify each caller's value in order to stratify service—in some situations this will mean offering low-value customers automated service and routing the high-value callers to a live domain expert.

Network Management

Network management software is used in multiswitch environments to distribute calls between sites based on routing rules established by the corporation. Network management software is an out-of-box CTI application that routes calls between the network and contact centers. The routing can be done in the network pre-arrival to the enterprise switch (also known as "in the cloud") or post-arrival in the contact center. Network-based routing is often used in addition to a premise-based CTI solution to increase the efficiency of call handling in a multisite contact center environment.

The Outbound Dialer

The dialer, also known as an outbound dialer, is a system that automates the initiation and dialing of outbound phone calls and connects calls to agents. Most dialers also include software that is able to identify when a call is picked up by an answering machine. Dialers work in two primary modes, predictive (also known as power dialing) and preview.

Using predictive dialing, the outbound system will make a large number of attempts and then connect customers who answer their phones to live agents. In this mode there is often a delay between the customer or prospect answering the phone and the agent saying hello. (The DNC provisions of the Federal Trade Commission's Telemarketing Sales Rule that went into effect in the fourth quarter of 2003 were intended to greatly reduce the number of "nuisance" calls, in which the person receiving the call answers but the dialer either doesn't connect quickly enough or disconnects because an agent is not available.)

The second primary dialing mode is preview. In preview mode, the person making the calls will first look at the account information and either dial the customer manually or push a button that dials the phone number. As agents are always present in this mode, it is not considered as disruptive as predictive dialing, but it is also nowhere near as cost effective. Dialers are predominantly used for telemarketing, collections, and fund raising.

Universal Queue

The universal queue (UQ) is essential for any multichannel contact center. The UQ functions as a funnel for all channels (phone, e-mail, and chat) and applies business rule workflow, routing, queuing, and data collection capabilities equally to all incoming transactions. A UQ is required if an organization wants to standardize its quality of service regardless of the channel through which a transaction arrives.

Operational Enhancements: Complementary Systems

In addition to core processing capabilities, there are many systems and applications that enhance the operation of contact centers. These solutions include

- Management systems: Performance management, workforce management, quality management, liability recording (logging), reporting, analytics (business intelligence), surveying, e-learning, real-time analytics, and speech analytics
- Supporting applications: Knowledge management (decision trees, case-based reasoning systems, neural net), content analysis, e-service, e-mail response management systems (ERMS), web self-service, scripting, letter writing, web-based chat, collaboration, and voice verification
- Front- and back-office applications: CRM suites, customer service and support tracking systems, sales systems, sales force automation, help desk systems, field service and dispatch systems, collections, human resources, enterprise resource planning, supply chain, and so on
- Enabling/common applications: Middleware, integration, extensible markup language (XML), security, workflow, databases, data marts, marketing encyclopedia, contracts, and configuration engines

Service Flexibility: Multichannel Support

The channels supported by contact centers include telephone, World Wide Web, handheld devices, wireless devices, fax, instant messaging, and video conferencing. The channels are a mix of voice and data-based media, adding complexity to the support infrastructure. Contact centers must seamlessly support the convergence of voice and data-based transactions to ensure that all channels receive the same level of service.

Role of Internet Protocol in Real-Time Contact Centers

Today, there are two primary communications networks—voice and data. For most of their history, contact centers processed calls over the public switched telephone network (PSTN) using circuit-based technology referred to as TDM. By and large, calls still move through the network and are processed by corporations this way, but IP is becoming increasingly popular.

IP was introduced in 1970 as a way of efficiently moving data between government and academic institutions to facilitate research. IP efficiently moves voice and data packets around the network. By the late 1990s, in conjunction with the Internet, voice-over IP (VoIP) was introduced as a method for bypassing the long-distance toll network. Voice-over IP enabled users of personal computers (PCs) to speak to each other over the data network. In its early days, the quality was bad but the price was right, as the calls were free.

Start-up carriers, like Global Crossing and Integrated Device Technology, Inc. (IDT), offered VoIP carrier-based services in competition with incumbent carriers like AT&T, MCI, and British Telecom, competing on price. The quality of VoIP improved in the last few years, as broadband connections became more common and opened up the market to increased use of IP.

Convergence was driving enterprises to integrate voice and data activities, and IP presented a vehicle for achieving this corporate goal. (It was assumed that integrating voice and data support would decrease IT support costs.) By 2001, the quality and performance of the new IP-based enterprise switches was adequate and early adopters began to implement them in corporations, though there was still room for improvement. But it took until 2003 before IP contact centers saw even limited market acceptance. More mainstream usage is expected in 2005.

Contact Center Internet Protocol Value Proposition

The primary value proposition for IP contact centers (and enterprise private business exchanges [PBXs], for that matter) is that they will reduce operating expenses by:

- Simplifying operating environments and support costs.
- Reducing toll charges.
- Facilitating multisite support.
- Eliminating the need for network management software.
- Standardizing the handling of voice and data transactions.

Internet protocol contact centers also facilitate the use of the UQ, remote agents, and hosted contact center support.

While the promise is real, until 2002, most IP-based contact center solutions were functionally limited, could not scale, and did not deliver the same rich capabilities as were found in the classic TDM-based contact center solutions. But the primary switch and contact center manufacturers (including Avaya, Nortel, and Siemens), stand-alone vendors (such as Aspect Communications Corporation), all-in-one or bundled suite players (including Apropos Technology Inc., Concerto Software, Inc., Cosmocom, Inc., and Interactive Intelligence Inc.) and contact center on demand (CCOD) companies (Cincom, Cisco Systems, Inc., Contactual, and Telephony@Work, Inc.), began to deliver new switches that were able to process voice and data-based transactions seamlessly, applying the same set of business rules, workflow, routing, and queuing rules to all transaction types. A number of these vendors fall into more than one category, with overlapping business models.

Vendors were highly motivated by enterprise demand for UQ-based offerings to simplify their operating environments and reporting requirements. IP gave them a way of accomplishing this goal, even though it required major changes to their products and a migration from hardware-based products to software-oriented solutions. See Figure 3.3.

Figure 3.3: Universal Queue

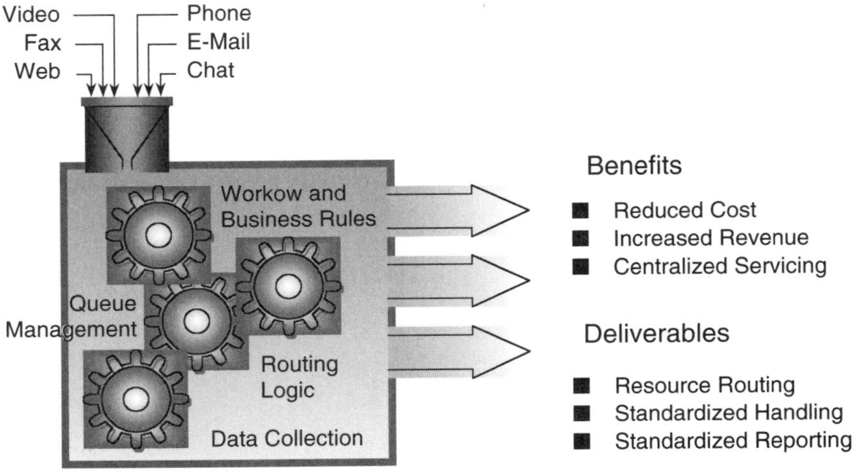

Source: Gartner.

Most companies do not yet utilize UQ and IP to their fullest and still have different processing streams for the different transaction types. The primary data transaction being delivered to contact centers is e-mail, although web-based chat, collaboration, and instant messaging (IM) are also in this category. And the market does not treat e-mails or chat sessions similarly to phone calls—calls are generally answered in 22 to 33 seconds (four to six rings), while it can take 3 to 5 minutes to answer a chat request and up to 24 hours to respond to an e-mail query. Customers want and deserve better service, and with UQ and IP enterprises will have the means of meeting and exceeding customer expectations.

Internet Protocol–Based Contact Centers: Viable, but Not Equal

The contact center infrastructure market was in turmoil between 2000 and 2003, when vendors were challenged to deliver software-based UQ and IP solutions. This upheaval, affecting both end users and vendors, has resulted in innovative and flexible products that are better positioned to grow with the enterprises they support.

Debates continue about the viability of IP-based contact center solutions, since the product offerings are not the same for all vendors. However, there are functionally rich IP-based contact center solutions currently available, and more are being delivered to the market. New start-up contact center sites, referred to as "greenfield," should invest in IP-based solutions that offer flexibility for the future without sacrificing functionality today.

Contact centers that are considering an upgrade should seriously consider migrating to IP and IP-enabled solutions, as long as doing so does not require a complete swap-out of all existing infrastructure (phone sets and other enterprise switches and ACDs). Internet protocol will add value to your organization in the future, but only compelling business reasons justify a complete swap-out of your existing telephony infrastructure.

Acquiring Appropriate Contact Center Infrastructure

Contact center managers have a great deal of choice in selecting a contact center model. They must consider technical, financial, and resource issues when determining the optimal direction for their business.

How to Pay for Your Contact Center: Financing Model

There are a growing number of contact center infrastructure solutions, and prospective buyers must address strategic issues even before carefully analyzing product functionality. You should begin by selecting the appropriate financing model for your company, as this will determine the range of products available for exploration and analysis. Investing in a new ACD, for example, can be expensive—ranging from less than $40K for a small system to millions of dollars for a multisite contact center.

Hosting is a viable option for companies that are either unable or unwilling to make a large up-front investment. As recently as a few years ago, enterprises that chose to host via the network or another application service provider (ASP) had to sacrifice functionality. This is no longer the case; network and ASP-based offerings are feature-rich today. The business model selection should be based on financials, timing, and staff availability. Enterprises should conduct an ROI analysis comparing the different options and select the one with the highest ROI and lowest total cost of ownership (TCO). There are three basic ways to acquire your core contact center infrastructure:

- *Purchase*. In this case, you acquire your own infrastructure. If you intend to use the same equipment for more than 3 years, it is almost always cheaper to purchase. This also gives you full control and in-house expertise. If you are in it for the long haul and can afford it, this is the way to go.
- *Rent/Host*. When you rent or host, you contract with a hosting company to provide access to the infrastructure you need. The advantages of hosting are that it can be implemented quickly and does not require your company to have or acquire a staff to support the equipment. The disadvantages are that (1) if you need the infrastructure for more than a year or two, it is usually cheaper to build it in-house, (2) you need to depend on outside expertise to optimize the environment as your requirements evolve, and (3) it may complicate your data security issues.
- *Lease*. Leasing contact center infrastructure is more like negotiating a financed purchase than a pure lease. The main reasons to lease rather than purchase are (1) you need a short-term (2 years or less) upgrade to an existing environment, (2) your firm has no cash available for a critical infrastructure investment, or (3) your firm has a very high after-tax cost of capital (15 percent or more). If you do lease, make sure that you have a

reasonably priced end-of-lease purchase option (preferably at a fixed price) in your contract. Otherwise, if you are not ready to replace your infrastructure exactly when your lease expires, you will likely overpay to extend the current lease.

Which Payment Option Is Right for You?

Here are a few guidelines for determining if your company should purchase, host, or lease:

1. If your company is planning on keeping the contact center for 5 years or longer, purchase is recommended.
2. If you already own other ACDs and can get a large discount by buying a new one (and will be keeping it for 3 years or longer), purchase is recommended.
3. If your cost of capital is low, generally within a couple of points of what you will be charged by the bank, and are planning to keep the technology for 3 to 4 years, purchase is recommended.
4. If you are putting up a temporary environment that will not be required after 12 months, hosting is recommended.
5. If you are going to greatly change your configuration and replace your initial investment in less than 2 years, hosting is recommended.
6. If you do not have technical resources to support the contact center, hosting is recommended.
7. If you do not have the cash to make the initial investment but still require the functionality for a high ROI, hosting is recommended.
8. If your company requires new or advanced ACD capabilities but does not want to carry the financial asset on its books or has a very high cost of capital, leasing may be the right choice.

Making the selection more complicated, it's possible to combine these financing models. For example, a company may choose to purchase a new contact center switch and then host it off-site for security or contingency reasons.

Selecting the Right Vendor

There are many established vendors and a few new ones in the contact center infrastructure market, as shown in Figure 3.4. The vendors and their

Figure 3.4: Contact Center Infrastructure Vendors

Category	Description	Vendors
Stand-Alone Contact Center Vendor	Vendors that service the contact center market only.	Aspect Communications
All-In-One/Bundled Suite Provider	Vendors that provide a bundled offering of contact center capabilities. Bundled products generally include ACD (and skill-based routing), UQ, CTI, IVR, and reporting.	Altitude Software, Apropos Technology, Inc., Concerto Software, Inc., Cosmocom, Inc., eON Communications Corporation, and Interactive Intelligence, Inc.
Primary Switch Manufacturers	Vendors that provide enterprise or carrier-grade switches in addition to contact center products.	Alcatel, Avaya, EADS Telecom, Ericsson, Mitel Networks Corporation, NEC Corporation, Nortel Networks, and Siemens AG
IP Only	Vendors that provide only IP-based contact center solutions.	Cisco Systems, Inc., CosmoCom, Inc., Nuasis Corporation, TelePhony@Work, Inc., and Wicom Communications Ltd.
Others	Vendors that provide contact center solutions.	Edify Corporation and Genesys Telecommunications Laboratories, Inc.
Hosted/On-Demand Technology Vendors	Vendors that provide hosted contact center capabilities.	Cisco Systems, Inc., CosmoCom, Inc., Lucent Client Care Division, Telephony@Work, Inc., and Wicom Communications Ltd.

Source: DMG Consulting LLC.

offerings are not equal, with substantial financial, practical, functional, technical, and vision differences among them. Functional differences are no longer directly related to a vendor's business model. The rapid techno-logical innovation of the past 3 years has resulted in new choices being de-livered to the market. When seeking a vendor, consider all vendors that can contribute to your organization's bottom line, but limit in-depth analyses to three to five vendors to keep the selection time frames reasonable.

After determining which vendors satisfy your organization's functional requirements, providers can be further differentiated based on many factors. The selection criteria should include vendor viability, financial strength, technology infrastructure, breadth of offerings, ability to integrate, use of standards, distribution model, systems integrator (SI) partnerships, mid-market strategy, support resources, R&D investments, and future plans. To streamline the selection process, develop an analytic framework that assigns weights to criteria, based on organizational needs. The information for the criteria can be gathered from industry analysts, web searches, consultants, or directly from the vendor, either in phone conversations or through a more formal request for information (RFI) or request for proposal (RFP) process.

Request for Proposal and Selection Process

Once three to five vendors are selected for detailed review, each should be invited to present its offering and product functionality. After the vendor presentation, either explain to or show each vendor the operating environment to ensure that the vendor proposes the right solution. After meeting with the vendors, draft and issue a detailed RFP that includes functional, technical, cost, and references sections. The RFP should require references that are similar to your organization's operating environment— for example, if your organization needs to integrate a logging system with an ACD, a vendor must have a proven ability to do this integration. If it turns out that none of the vendors have the required experience, they can be invited to a lab (or your organization's operating environment) to demonstrate their capabilities before proceeding to the next phase of the selection process. This will slow down the selection process and may cost a few dollars, but the time and cost saved during implementation will rapidly cover these up-front investments.

Once you have identified at least two vendors who can meet your organization's needs, select the least-cost provider through a competitive bidding process. Near-term needs must be addressed at this stage. Some vendors give a low bid to get in the door and then raise their costs for add-on hardware and future support services. Future pricing and all service expectations in the contract should also be addressed. The agreement should not be signed until all issues are addressed to your satisfaction. Once the agreement is signed, you lose all negotiating power.

Contact Center Integration Requirements

The primary system in any contact center is the ACD, which must therefore easily integrate with other applications and technologies, particularly those that were in place before the ACD was purchased. Although all vendors will claim that their ACD is easy to integrate, this is often not the case. Buying an all-in-one/bundled solution can minimize—but does not solve—the challenge because the ACD still needs to be integrated with the company's customer information or sales system(s).

As recently as 2001, some ACD vendors believed that their system was "king" of the contact center and that all other technology components needed to integrate with it. Their approach was to publish an application programming interface (API) and leave the integration to others. During the past couple of years, most ACD vendors have changed their attitude and enhanced their integration strategies and capabilities, but there still are some holdouts whose technology limits ease of integration.

During the IP transition, the more forward-thinking vendors developed non-proprietary, standards-based applications that included a web services integration strategy. While standards-based integration will reduce integration costs and challenges, it's also important to select a vendor with out-of-box APIs for the systems that need to be integrated. (Vendors list all existing APIs on their price list. If it's not on the list, it hasn't been built.) The use of web services will reduce the time spent on custom integration efforts by at least 60 percent, but it's still best to avoid any customized development.

Security and Backup

As contact centers are the focal point for customer interactions, ensuring that service is not disrupted by an act of God, a power interruption, weather, terrorism, or hackers is paramount. The contact center must include security that controls all systems, user modules, and functions. It must also adhere to the security requirements of the enterprise, which include Microsoft Service Packs and virus protection software (Norton or McAfee, for example) if its server is Microsoft-based. The security staff should be invited to participate in the selection process and review your current systems environment to ensure that service disruptions can be minimized, if not completely prevented.

Most contact center vendors claim overall reliability of 99.9 percent. Reliability is a general number that reflects system availability and mean time between failures. While this means that the systems are generally dependable, it's essential to have backup in place to protect against the inevitable 0.01 percent chance of failure, unless you can afford to be out of service for an indefinite period of time. All of the systems include backup options and features that will vary in price. It's important to analyze a company's needs and balance the impact of a system outage with the incremental cost of adding backup hardware and software. Too many companies make this investment only after their first failure.

System and Application Requirements

System requirements will vary dramatically based on the size, purpose, and complexity of each contact center. System needs will also change during the life of a contact center, as organizations evolve. For example, system requirements for a 50-seat contact center are different from those of a 250-seat department.

However, system requirements are not the only factor in investment decisions. Instead, the primary concerns for most companies are cost and complexity. Return on investment is generally the primary decision criterion for organizations of all sizes, small, mid-size, and large; however, practical issues play an important role. If a small company does not have the money to make an investment, a great ROI will not help. Return on investment and the TCO, which is the total cost of implementing and supporting a technology investment over the life of the asset, are the primary financial measures used for evaluating technology investments. System complexity is addressed by the TCO, as this measure will increase if the system is difficult to support and maintain.

Four Key Technology Factors to Consider *Before* Purchase

Typically, there are four factors that determine the technology and system requirements for a contact center:

1. *Size:* The volume of transactions (calls, e-mails, chat sessions, faxes) to be handled by the department

2. *Purpose:* The function of the contact center; for example, sales, customer service, collections, fraud, help desk, human resources
3. *Channels:* The media through which transactions will be processed, such as phone, e-mail, chat, collaboration, IM, fax
4. *Call Direction:* The flow of transactions; that is, inbound/outbound/both

Size

Small contact centers (20 or fewer agents) require some form of an ACD to manage calls and e-mails. Most small centers would also benefit from an IVR, preferably one that is speech-enabled so that it can be used both as a call router and to free agents from tasks that do not require live assistance. Besides reporting, most small contact centers do not require other management tools and can be run on instinct and spreadsheets. Some management tools, such as workforce management, quality management, and surveying, would benefit a small contact center as much as a large one, but they are not cost effective. (Liability recording may be a federal requirement if the contact center is involved in sales activities.)

Every contact center will require some kind of front-office application or customer system so that agents can either process sales or address inquiries. In basic contact centers, the front-office application may be "stand-alone," meaning that it is used only by the contact center and is not integrated with other systems in the company. However, while a stand-alone front-office application is less expensive, the value of the contact center to the rest of the company increases if its supporting system is integrated and shared with other operating areas.

Purpose and Channels

Small Contact Centers

Along with its size, a contact center's purpose and channels also affect its system requirements. If the contact center is a help desk or handles complex system inquiries, it will benefit greatly from a knowledge management (KM) system. If a small contact center predominantly handles e-mail inquiries, then an ERMS would be helpful. However, the small size of these centers means that many activities can be handled adequately by homegrown or existing tools, such as a standard e-mail package. Small contact centers do not require any of the enabling or common applications described in Figure 3.2 above.

Mid-Size Contact Centers

Mid-size contact centers have 21 to 75 agents. The basic rule is that contact centers with less than 50 agents can operate with just an ACD, a front-office processing system, reporting, and best practices, as managers can supervise what they can easily see. This doesn't mean that a mid-size contact center with less than 50 agents wouldn't benefit from management and supporting systems, just that it can get by without them. Once a contact center grows beyond 50 agents, it's time to consider new investments to automate and simplify the management challenge.

Like a small contact center, a mid-size contact center with more than 50 agents requires an ACD with advanced routing capabilities, a front-office processing system, a speech-enabled IVR, and, of course, reporting. Mid-size contact centers will also benefit from quality management and surveying software—so they can constantly measure the pulse of their customers. These systems are important for smaller organizations, as they have fewer customers and cannot afford to lose any of them. If the contact center is involved in selling, a liability recording system will have to be installed to comply with a number of legislative requirements.

Supporting system requirements for mid-size contact centers are driven by the department's purpose, just as they are for contact centers of all sizes. Knowledge management will benefit any contact center that provides detailed technical support, such as a help desk or a health care company. Web self-service is a great way of empowering customers to help themselves and, if well designed, will reduce the volume of calls to live agents. Scripting software can streamline the delivery of information to customers, improve call quality, streamline inbound or outbound environments, and be very helpful in a mid-size contact center that cannot afford to spend money on agent training.

Real-time analytics and speech analytics are beneficial for contact centers of all sizes, including mid-size centers. As both of these applications capture, analyze, and structure customer communications, they allow organizations to deliver products and services that best satisfy customers and also address operational issues. Real-time analytics takes service to the next level, allowing the contact center to engage customers at the point of contact and leverage every customer transaction.

Mid-size contact centers that support data transactions (e-mail, chat, IM, collaboration) may require systems such as an ERMS for e-mail handling and an e-service application to address chat, collaboration, and IM. If a mid-size contact center predominantly supports electronic channels, then it will benefit and realize a rapid ROI from an e-service suite. If electronic channel support is incidental, then these systems will not add a great deal of value.

Large Contact Centers

Once a contact center has more than 100 agents, system requirements increase and become more complex. Large contact centers include 76 to 400 seats, and their system requirements change as the number of agents increases. Another major factor is the number of sites that are part of the contact center environment.

In general, large contact centers require an ACD, IVR, CTI, UQ, and integrated reporting. If the center is a multisite environment without IP, network management is essential for maintaining productivity. Large contact centers require front-office systems that are integrated with the enterprise's other operating systems. It is ideal to use a CRM suite, whether purchased or homegrown, and there is value in tying the front-office systems with the company's ERP and supply-chain environments to give the company a 360-degree view of customer activities.

In contact centers with more than 100 agents, workforce management and quality management become essential. Liability recording may already be necessary, but even if not legislated, could add value. Surveying software is always nice to have but is still not viewed as a requirement, although it can give a contact center of any size a strategic advantage. E-learning, real-time analytics, and speech analytics continue to be "nice to haves" in contact centers of all sizes. However, as centers grow in size the potential benefits and ROI from these management applications increase.

Performance management software is a necessity for large contact centers with more than 250 agents, but it may have a rapid payback even in centers with as few as 100 agents. Performance management is valuable because it enhances all contact center activities.

As in all contact centers, the supporting system requirements are driven by each organization's purpose. If the contact center supports a field service department, then it will require a field service and dispatch system to operate effectively. If the department is doing collections, then it will need a system that allows it to reflect payments and promise-to-pay activities.

Using enabling systems begins to make financial sense once a contact center has grown to between 100 and 250 agents. Enabling systems, such as a marketing encyclopedia, can be useful in contact centers of all sizes. But these investments become cost effective only if the expense can be distributed among a large volume of transactions. And of course, each organization should use only the applications that are required to support its specific business needs.

Very Large Contact Centers

System requirements for very large contact centers (more than 250 agents) are similar to those for large contact centers. The ROI from technology investments is often much more rapid in larger centers, as the costs are distributed among a greater volume of transactions. This is why it's much easier for a large or very large contact center to justify and make investments in technology. It is for this reason that vendors have traditionally concentrated on selling to the larger centers. However, as there are few new large and very large contact centers being built in North America, vendors are following the money to the mid-size market.

Call Direction

Contact centers that make outbound calls and have at least 50 agents require some kind of outbound dialing system. If the contact center handles inbound and outbound transactions, then it will also benefit from call-blending software. This technology manages inbound and outbound transaction queues to optimize the use of all agents.

Contact Center Infrastructure Best Practices Checklist

Following best practices will help you realize the greatest benefit as quickly as possible from all contact center investments. Use the following checklist to maximize the payoff of your investments.

❑ Calculate the ROI and TCO for all potential contact center investments.

❑ Whether yours is a new or growing contact center, invest only in tools that have an ROI that meets your corporate guidelines and

---

have an acceptable TCO. If you do not have ROI guidelines, it's suggested that all contact center investments pay for themselves within 3 to18 months, with the exception of the ACD, which should have a 2- to 3-year payback.

❏ Prioritize system requirements and continuously review your priorities. There are a lot of helpful and beneficial systems and applications available, but few contact centers can buy them all.

❏ Buy only what you need. Don't let vendors convince you to make investments for uncertain future growth. Contact center needs change rapidly and often unexpectedly.

❏ Make sure that you have resources, whether internal or external, to implement and support the technologies that you want before making an investment.

❏ Before making any contact center investments, check to make sure that the system(s) under consideration can be easily integrated with applications already installed.

❏ If a vendor hasn't proven its ability to integrate with one or more systems in your operating environment, make the deal contingent upon a successful test or full integration. (It's preferable to run a test in a lab, if possible.)

❏ Involve all levels of contact center staff in technology selections. Agents, supervisors, managers, and technical staff will each bring different and helpful perspectives to the selection process.

❏ Communicate early and frequently with contact center staff about system changes to get their buy-in and support.

❏ Provide training for each new system. This ensures that you will quickly realize the benefits of the application.

4

The Power of Speech Recognition for Self-Service

Self-service functionality, including web-based self-service, IVRs, and, increasingly, speech recognition, has become indispensable to contact centers of all sizes. Even small contact centers are using voice prompters or call routers (which are essentially basic IVR systems) to improve the efficiency of call handling.

Self-Service:
From Cost-Saving Necessity to Customer Requirement

While the value proposition of a well-designed, well-implemented, and well-communicated self-service application is high for companies and their customers (see Figure 4.1), too many enterprises make the mistake of prioritizing their own wants over their customers' needs when building these systems. This classic misstep has plagued each generation of self-service technologies, causing many initiatives to fail on their first attempt.

What's amazing is that at each stage of development of self-service systems—web-based self-service, touchtone IVR, and speech recognition—contact centers have had to relearn the fundamental concept of putting the customer first. Once this challenge was addressed, the benefits have proven to be great for customers and enterprises alike and the payback as rapid as 3 months.

Figure 4.1: Median Cost per Transaction (by channel)

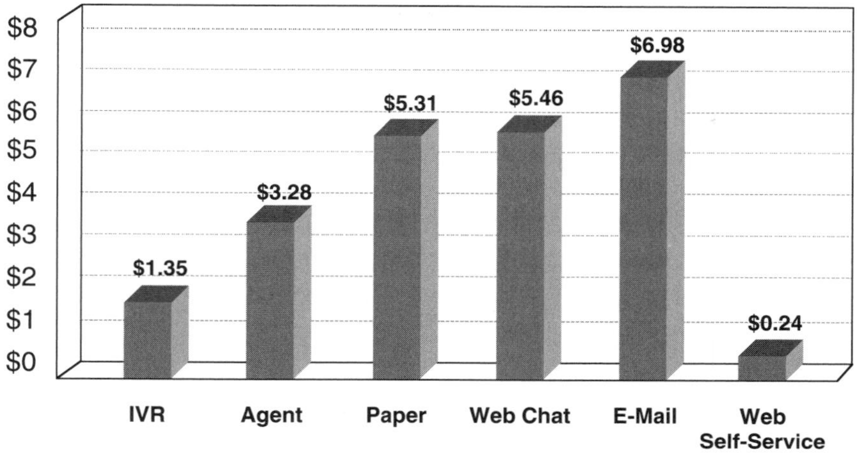

Source: Gartner, Fall 2003.

Adapting Service to Changing Customer Behavior

Customers must be allowed to use their channel of choice, even when it is not the preferred medium for the enterprise. For example, the cost of using live agents to respond to basic "What's my balance?" inquiries is prohibitively high, and this is a type of transaction where agents do not add a great deal of value. While companies cannot force customers to use less expensive self-service channels unless they are willing to risk losing them, they absolutely can and should motivate clients to use alternative channels. As an incentive, companies should offer pricing discounts and enhanced service to customers who do make the move. It's essential for an enterprise to deliver on its promises in these alternative channels. So, if you promise additional or speedier service for customers who use self-service, make sure customers feel rewarded for their decision. Otherwise, they'll use the self-service application once and very likely return to the more expensive phone and agent-based service. For example, if you entice customers to a self-service web site with promises of less expensive products, be sure to offer discounted items of equal or higher quality than what the customer could obtain through traditional channels.

Speech Recognition Is Ready for Prime Time

After 20-plus years, billions of dollars in investments, and many false starts, speech recognition technology, including the new standardized out-of-box packaged applications, is ready for deployment in companies of all sizes—small, medium, and large—and for all risk profiles—risk takers, mainstream system users, and risk-averse organizations. Both companies with large and sophisticated DTMF (also known as touch-tone IVR) environments (see Figure 4.2) and those just beginning to consider IVR-based self-service can realize great benefits from speech recognition applications. In the next 3 to 5 years, the market is expected to deliver many outstanding, innovative, and flexible web-based self-service and speech recognition applications.

The results of speech recognition implementations will vary based on many criteria, including application relevancy, application design and interface, business complexity, customer base, and how well the application

Figure 4.2: Typical DTMF Utilization Rates

Industry	Purpose	Examples	DTMF Call Completion Ranges
Financial Services	Informational	Account balances, stock quotes, branch locations	40% to 90%
	Transactional	Transferring funds, making payments, credit line increases, stock purchases, collections	25% to 65%
Insurance	Informational	Health care coverage, list of doctors in a plan, claim verifications	20% to 60%
	Transactional	Making payments, challenging claims	20% to 45%
Travel	Informational	Schedules, arrival and departure times, checking loyalty program status	35% to 65%
	Transactional	Reservations, booking seats, reporting lost luggage	25% to 60%
Utilities	Informational and Transactional	Billing information, payments, turning service on/off	10% to 20%

Source: DMG Consulting LLC.

is communicated and maintained. There are general guidelines, however, for projecting usage rates. (See Figure 4.3.)

If a company's touch-tone IVR usage rate is below 20 percent, then (1) touch-tone IVR is not an appropriate application for this customer base, or (2) the system does not provide the functionality required by its customers, or (3) the system is poorly designed or communicated. When there is a mismatch between system capabilities and the implementation, the potential benefits of adding speech capabilities are generally greater than for organizations that have already done an adequate job of leveraging touch-tone IVR usage. But, when considering adding speech recognition technology to an environment where there is either no existing touch-tone IVR or there is one that is not well received, with usage rates below 20 percent, it's essential to determine at the outset if speech is going to be received any better. (See sidebar on "Speech Recognition Best Practices.")

Figure 4.3: Projected Speech Recognition Usage Rates

Current Touch-Tone Usage Rate	Projected Increase with Speech Recognition	New Usage Rate
Below 20%	80% to 150%	34% to 48%
20% to 30%	45% to 100%	29% to 60%
31% to 45%	40% to 50%	43% to 68%
Above 45%	10% to 30%	50% to 80%

Source: DMG Consulting LLC.

Benefits of Speech Recognition

There have been significant developments in the IVR world since 1999, especially in speech recognition. During the past 4 years, the speech recognition engines themselves have improved, with huge strides in technology usability being the most substantial contributions to this market. In 1999, users investing in a speech implementation were more than likely to fail in their first attempt because the applications were difficult to use. Now, the chances for success are as great as the likely payback.

Speech Recognition Best Practices

Applying best practices and lessons learned from the thousands of existing speech recognition implementations will lead to a successful initiative. The recommendations provided here will help your enterprise avoid common pitfalls and build a speech environment that your customers will find compelling and useful. The most important step is to hire speech recognition experts if speech is new to your organization and you do not have voice dialogue experts on staff. Experience with DTMF applications is not adequate preparation for building a speech interface; neither is it enough to take a course or two on the topic. Effective speech recognition applications require years of hands-on experience. Here are best practices for building a successful speech recognition application.

1. Conduct a customer needs assessment before making investments. Too many companies skip this step in order to save money, assuming that their service and marketing organization will take care of this detail or that customers will just use whatever they provide.
2. Hire speech recognition experts to assist with the implementation.
3. Give customers what they want in the speech application, not what your enterprise would like them to want. Customers want to do business their way and will use the system only if they find it valuable.
4. Involve agents in system design and testing. Contact center agents generally know what customers want and are the most appropriate internal group to represent the needs of customers.
5. Invest in the voice user interface, dialogue design, system persona, and voice. These components are critical to your company's branding, voice experience, and success of the application.
6. Keep dialogues succinct and simple, and use proper language. Do not overwhelm customers with too many options. Speech is a very simple interface, but if too many options are presented, customers will get confused and request agent assistance.
7. Allow customers to access live agents easily. Customers do not want to feel trapped in the system. If they can easily reach a live agent, they are more likely to give the system a try.

8. Create a customer feedback loop and closely monitor customer preferences. Create an environment that allows customers to share their thoughts with your company and then take advantage of that input.
9. Quickly fix problems identified by customers and enhance the speech application on a periodic basis. Do not make major adjustments to the application, user interface, and dialogue more than once a quarter, though, as customers do not like frequent change, even if they do want enhancements.
10. Communicate with customers about service enhancements. Do not wait for customers to stumble upon options in the speech application.
11. Involve all customer-facing departments, including sales and marketing, in the speech effort. The speech system benefits the entire organization, not just the service department.

Hard Benefits:
Financial Reasons to Invest in Speech Recognition

Contact center managers should justify speech recognition investments based on the following "hard" benefits, as these categories will be approved by chief financial officers (CFOs), who are carefully watching how investments are justified:

1. *Productivity Improvements.* Reducing the need for additional agents, supervisors, trainers, and quality assurance specialists. Keep in mind that many organizations are continuing to hire new agents, so it's unlikely that current staff will lose their jobs. Instead, speech recognition should keep a company's hiring needs at a moderate level.
2. *Cost Reduction.* Decreasing the number of calls, agent talk time, line charges, and hiring and training costs.
3. *Cost Avoidance.* Eliminating the need to purchase more hardware or software to handle additional calls. If a call center is maxed out, this savings could also involve avoiding the cost of building a new center.

Soft Benefits:
Indirect Gains from Investment in Speech Recognition

The soft benefits that enterprises should consider when making a speech recognition system selection are:

1. *Reduced Number of Abandoned Calls.* When the call volume is high and customers have to wait a long time, they often hang up and call back. This increases a company's line charges and hurts customer satisfaction.
2. *Fewer Customer Callbacks.* If customers are satisfied the first time they call, they will not need to call back.
3. *Reduction in Agent Attrition.* Agents prefer handling challenging inquiries to dealing with routine ones that do not require much thought. Using a speech-enabled IVR to handle mundane inquiries will increase agent job satisfaction.
4. *Increased Customer Satisfaction.* Customers want answers and they want them quickly, accurately, and in their frame of reference. Touchtone IVR is effective for providing basic information, but not for addressing complex inquiries or activities that require a great deal of customer input. Speech recognition software will improve the operation of some complex touch-tone IVR scripts and allow companies to provide services not previously possible with touch-tone IVR, bolstering customer satisfaction and encouraging usage of the system.
5. *Increased Customer Loyalty.* If customers are happy with service quality, they will have no reason to go elsewhere. Freed by automation from many monotonous calls, agents will have more patience for complex inquiries that require live assistance.
6. *Increased Revenue.* Speech recognition can be used on both an inbound and outbound basis to generate incremental revenue.

These soft benefits are real but are often difficult to quantify and hard to attribute directly to the speech system. Still, soft benefits should be considered when deciding if speech recognition is appropriate for your operating environment, even though the core financial justification and ROI analysis should be based on hard dollar savings.

Speech Recognition Return on Investment

Investments in speech recognition systems typically yield a payback of less than 12 months from the time of implementation. In order to track and report the success of any project, including a speech initiative, conduct a baseline analysis of the operating area or function prior to making an investment. This way, you will be able to accurately measure the success of the implementation and determine whether it produced the projected savings.

Reducing operating expenses and improving productivity and service quality are requirements for all contact centers. In the ROI model for the hypothetical company in Figure 4.4, the cost per DTMF handled call was $0.45, 91 percent lower than the $5.00 per agent-handled call. Therefore, the contact center wanted to improve its phone-based self-service solutions. After analyzing its options, the enterprise chose to introduce speech technology to improve the ease of use and navigation of the existing DTMF system and to provide new functionality. After analyzing customer needs, the current DTMF-based system was enhanced and customers allowed to use the speech recognition application to change their names and addresses in a secure environment, use touch-tone data entry to obtain complex information that they couldn't previously request on the phone, and have access to all the standard functions (e.g., obtaining information, requesting balances, making payments, scheduling appointments, and placing orders).

The numbers used in the model in Figure 4.4 are typical of many service organizations in the financial services, utilities, insurance, and travel industries. This company pays $0.04 per minute for its phone service and had a 25 percent customer completion rate from its touch-tone-based IVR prior to introducing speech. The model reflects the financial benefits of introducing speech recognition technology into a customer service contact center that receives 5 million calls per year, has an average agent talk time of 4 minutes, an IVR talk time of 2 minutes, a 90-second wait time, and a cost of $5.00 per agent-handled call. (This model can be used as a guide but must be adjusted for each investment, as savings will vary by site even within organizations.)

Figure 4.4: Speech Recognition ROI Model for ABC Corp.

Assumptions		Baseline	Year 1	Year 2	Year 3
Total incoming calls		5,000,000	5,000,000	5,250,000	5,512,500
Touch-tone IVR automation %		25	25	25	25
Automation % uplift from adding speech		0	11	14	16
Incremental automated call volume		N/A	562,500	721,875	895,781
Average agent talk time (minutes)	4.0				
Average talk time of speech IVR (minutes)	2.0				
Average talk time of DTMF IVR (minutes)	2.0				
Average hold time for agent calls (minutes)	1.5				
Toll-free cost/minute	$0.04				
Cost per agent-handled call	$5.00				
Expenses					
One-Time Investments					
DTMF ports (hardware/software)	$48,000				
Speech ports (software)	$76,800				
Development, implementation, and integration costs	$200,000				
Total one-time investments	$324,800				
Annual Costs					
Incremental DTMF ports (hardware/software)			$—	$—	$48,000
Incremental speech ports (software)			$—	$—	$19,200
Follow-on software development			$125,000	$100,000	$—
In-house support (1 FTE)			$100,000	$100,000	$100,000
DTMF port maintenance (18%)			$8,640	$8,640	$17,280
Speech port maintenance (18%)			$13,824	$13,824	$17,280
Total annual costs			$247,464	$222,464	$134,560

Benefits			
Displaced calls from live agents	$2,812,500	$3,609,375	$4,478,906
Reduced call length	$45,000	$57,750	$71,663
Reduced call hold time	$33,750	$43,313	$53,747
Total annual savings	$2,891,250	$3,710,438	$4,604,316
Return on Investment			
Payback period (months)	1.5		
Net Present Value (NPV) (3 years @12%)	$7,997,798		
Internal Rate of Return (IRR)	843%		

Source: DMG Consulting LLC.

The investment in speech recognition required $324,800 in start-up costs in year zero. Start-up costs included:

- 12 additional IVR ports at a cost of $4,000 per port for hardware and software.
- 48 speech ports at a cost of $1,600 per port.
- $200,000 for developing, implementing, and integrating the voice user interface. This cost also covers the fee for "voice talent."

Speech Recognition Costs

The most common way to implement speech recognition technology is to add it to a touch-tone IVR system. The model in Figure 4.4 reflects a one-to-one relationship between touch-tone IVR and speech ports. As the speech software sits on top of the touch-tone IVR hardware, there are no incremental hardware costs when speech software is added. The costs for a speech recognition application are reflected in Figure 4.5.

The incremental costs of handling the increasing call volume, developing new software, and internal and external support were $247,464, $222,464, and $134,560 respectively in years one through three. The payback from adding speech to the DTMF environment was 1.5 months. This investment had a net present value of $7,997,798, and the internal rate of return was 843 percent over 3 years. This investment contributed $2.9 million to the company's pre-tax bottom line during its first year.

The DTMF and speech port requirements are calculated based on a contact center's busy hour call volume. Interactive voice response software

Figure 4.5: Speech Recognition Cost Estimates

Category	Cost	Comments
Cost per Speech Port	From $200, for a very basic system, to $1,600 for advanced natural language recognition capabilities	Expect to have to purchase a minimum of 12 ports
Application Development	From $35,000, for a basic auto attendant application, to more than $500,000 for a sophisticated application	Costs can be reduced by using an out-of-box application from a Voice ASP
Cost per DTMF IVR Port	From $600 to $1500, depending on the size of the system	In service environments, the majority of speech recognition applications are implemented in conjunction with an existing touch-tone IVR

Source: DMG Consulting LLC.

is sold in increments of 12, so this model rounded the required number of ports up to the nearest multiple of 12. With a baseline 25 percent DTMF utilization rate, only 30 ports were needed to handle the IVR touch-tone volume. The IVR usage rose from 25 to 36 percent, a 45 percent increase, when speech recognition software was added to the environment. This increased the DTMF and speech port requirements to 41. Year one also included an investment of $125,000 in software. In year two, an additional $100,000 was spent to enhance the application's capabilities and use of the speech-enabled IVR increased to 55 percent, bringing the port requirements to 45. By the end of year three, the utilization rate had risen to 65 percent above the original usage, increasing the DTMF and speech port requirements to 50.

Cost Savings of Speech Recognition

Speech recognition software can benefit most enterprises, whether or not they have an existing touch-tone IVR system. If the call volume is high enough, even a company that already realizes an 80 percent touch-tone IVR utilization rate may get a rapid payback for speech recognition. Figure 4.6 shows four companies where the investment yielded annual savings of more than $1 million.

Figure 4.6: Increasing Self-Help and Cost Savings with Speech Recognition

Company	Amtrak Train Status[a]	Dreyfus[b]	Merrill Lynch[b]	Michigan Department of Treasury[a]
Touch-Tone IVR Usage Rate	42%	45%	82%	10%
Usage Rate After Speech Recognition Implementation	70%	63%	90%	98% (tax refund status calls)
Call Volume	2.8 million/year	12,000/day	50 million/year	2 million/year
Annual Savings	~$1.2 million	~$1 million	$6.3 million	$ 2 million

a. *Source:* ScanSoft.
b. *Source:* Nuance.

Expanding Self-Service with Speech Recognition

Speech recognition applications take two primary forms: contact center applications (referred to as enterprise applications) and embedded applications, where a speech recognition application is part of another system, such as a cell phone or automobile. As speech is the most ubiquitous, comfortable, and preferred form of communication for enterprise customers, the uses of speech technology are quickly expanding beyond contact centers. Possibilities include the following:

- *Automotive:* Directions, emergency assistance, basic car instructions, and navigation systems
- *Content:* Stock quotes, news, sports, weather, and horoscopes
- *Retail:* Placing orders, obtaining price quotes, checking availability of stock items, locating stores, getting addresses and directions
- *Telcos:* Voice-activated dialing, information portals, phone-based e-mail readers, directory and operator assistance
- *Advertising:* Permission-based advertisements to fill time spent waiting for service representatives
- *Collections:* Promise-to-pay and commitments
- *Government:* Loan applications, checking the status of filed documents, locating post offices or other government buildings, directions, ordering forms
- *Transportation:* Train and airplane schedules, booking travel reservations, changing or canceling reservations, checking airplane or train status,

complaints about lost luggage, ordering special meals, seat selection, and checking status of loyalty programs

- *Field Service:* Checking availability and status of parts, ordering parts, scheduling service visits
- *Entertainment:* Identifying location of movies or shows, making dinner reservations, purchasing tickets, and getting directions
- *Credit Card:* Authenticating callers, obtaining account balances and available credit, making payments, transferring funds, requesting statement copies, verifying receipt of new cards, card activations, reporting lost and stolen cards, new marketing promotions, credit line increases
- *Sales Force* Automation: Placing orders, scheduling follow-up visits, and service requests
- *Insurance:* Verifying medical coverage and checking status of payments and refunds
- *Parcel Service:* Requesting a pickup or supplies, checking package status, office locations and directions, rate calculations, lost item reporting
- *Energy:* Meter tracking, turning service on and off, balance information, making payments, checking payment due dates, reporting gas leaks
- *Contact Center:* Product and service information, making payments, placing orders, reviewing order status, updating personal information, name and address changes, applying for credit, applying for jobs, locating stores, libraries, or hospitals, pricing information, scheduling appointments, marketing promotions

Extending the reach of self-service is an increasing priority for enterprises that now require costly agent handling for many transactions. In the future, as automated speech conversations become more like natural language, applications will expand to activities as complex as customer retention.

Speech Recognition Application Development Standards: Paving the Way for Future Growth

For most of their history, speech applications were platform-dependent, meaning that an application had to be built on a specific platform. This restricted vendors from developing a generic speech application, such as one providing account balance information, and selling it to any company that needed access to account data. As all early speech applications had to be customized for each business, developing speech recognition applications was prohibitively expensive for all but a limited number of companies.

In 1998, Motorola, AT&T, IBM, Lucent, and a few other companies collaborated to introduce the first open speech standard, voice extensible markup language (voiceXML), to the market. The idea behind VXML, as it is commonly called, was to enable developers to build speech applications without knowing anything about the hardware that the application was going to run on. The concept was great, and the application was good enough for basic use, opening up new avenues to both vendors and users. But early versions of VXML were immature and missing essential functionality, such as call control, limiting its use and market acceptance in complex environments. VoiceXML standards are the responsibility of the World Wide Web Consortium (W3C), and a number of working groups are actively addressing and improving this markup language.

VoiceXML is the de facto standard for speech applications today. It is still maturing but does deliver on its promise of platform-independent speech applications, even if it isn't yet perfect. Many vendors are offering VXML development environments to simplify the delivery of speech applications. Other vendors have out-of-box speech applications that can be purchased and easily customized.

Few markets have a single standard, and the speech market place is no exception. In February 2001 the Speech Application Language Tags Forum (SALT) was founded. SALT, like VXML, is a development language for speech applications. According to the Forum, SALT "enables multimodal and telephony-enabled access to information, applications, and Web services from PCs, telephones, table PCs and personal digital assistants (PDAs)." SALT is the cornerstone of Microsoft's speech platform and, while not widely used as of April 2005, cannot be counted out. If Microsoft puts its marketing muscle behind its new speech initiative, SALT will likely become a more common standard.

The two contending standards represent great innovation for the speech recognition marketplace and the competition is expected to speed up the rate of innovation in the market. New out-of-box applications are being delivered to the market at an increasing rate, as are VXML development environments that facilitate development and introduction of speech recognition solutions. Standards-based application development has already reduced the cost of speech applications by 25 to 35 percent, and as newer boxed applications come to market the costs are expected to drop further. Now is a great time to get into this market and take advantage of the improved tools and decreasing costs.

Neither standard is perfect, but VXML is more than adequate for all but extremely complex applications (which may still require cutting back to a proprietary IVR development tool). The limitations are being addressed by the W3C and, with SALT on its heels, expect to see speedier delivery of improved standards. Speech recognition prospects should invest only in applications that use VXML (or SALT, if so inclined), as this is where the innovation is going to take place in the next few years.

The Speech Recognition Market

This market has seen many vendors come and go during the past 20 years. New vendors are expected to enter the market with packaged speech recognition offerings, now that the VoiceXML and SALT standards are mature enough to allow platform-independent application development. The speech recognition market now has four groups: the primary technology providers, platform providers, ASPs, and network providers. There is a significant amount of crossover between these groups. The primary technology providers include AT&T, IBM, Microsoft, Nuance, ScanSoft/SpeechWorks, and Philips. The platform providers are vendors that offer a server intended for touch-tone and speech applications. (The majority of these vendors started as touch-tone IVR providers and have added speech to their platforms.) These vendors include Aspect Communications Corporation, Avaya, Cisco Systems, Inc., Computer Talk Technology, Inc., Edify Corporation, Genesys Telecommunications Laboratories, Inc., IBM, Interactive Intelligence, Inc., Intervoice, Inc., Microsoft, Nortel Networks, Nuance, and Syntellect, Inc. (a division of Enghouse Systems Limited). ASPs include BeVocal, Inc., Convergys Corporation, Datatel Communications, IBM, NetbyTel Inc., TellMe Networks Inc., VoiceGenie Technologies Inc., and West Corporation. Packaged application vendors provide solutions that can be premise-based or hosted. These vendors are Apptera, Datria Systems, Inc., Fluency Voice Technology Ltd., Harborlight Technologies LLC, Metaphor Solutions Inc., and Tu-Vox Incorporated. The network providers offer IVR capabilities from within their networks. These vendors include carriers such as AT&T, BT, and MCI and some of the outsourcers, including Convergys Corporation and West Corporation.

Getting Started with Speech Recognition

A large number of vendors are selling excellent speech recognition technology and applications today. What remains limited and drives up the cost of speech applications is development of the voice dialogue and user interface. During the next few years, the market will see many new out-of-box speech applications that will reduce the cost and development time for speech systems. But if the application you want isn't yet available, be sure to purchase a product with a VXML development environment to ease the development burden.

Speech Recognition Implementation Checklist

Follow the steps in the following checklist to make sure that the project is a success for you, your company, and your customers. As with any investment, determine the return on investment before making any purchase decisions. Follow the steps in order.

- ❏ Identify business needs.
- ❏ Obtain corporate technology investment guidelines.
- ❏ Identify project sponsor and set up cross-functional project team.
- ❏ Determine technical requirements, including integration needs.
- ❏ Document functional and technical requirements.
- ❏ Issue RFI (optional) and RFP.
- ❏ Assess RFP responses.
- ❏ Compare investment options (ROI: payback, NPV, and IRR).
- ❏ Incorporate soft benefits into the analysis.
- ❏ Make selection.
- ❏ Benchmark operating area prior to implementing new technology.
- ❏ Reflect responsibilities and deliverables in contract.
- ❏ Draft detailed project plan.
- ❏ Measure project success.
- ❏ Communicate project success.

5

Designing, Building, and Maintaining a Vibrant E-Service Strategy

Internet-based customer service (also known as e-service or web-based self-service) has evolved since the mid-1990s, when it was considered an afterthought of e-commerce, to an essential element of every company's customer service and CRM strategy today. It would be great to think the maturity and expansion of this sector of the software market is the result of companies recognizing the value e-service offers to customers. The reality, though, is that this market has grown because of pressure on enterprises to reduce sales and service costs by minimizing human-assisted transactions. But don't expect less emphasis on e-service in a stronger economy; the e-service sector of CRM showed signs of strength as early as 2002 and appears poised to grow as the economy improves. Moreover, the e-service phenomenon is presenting challenges to the CRM industry status quo, with upstarts such as RightNow competing seriously against market giant Siebel and garnering the attention of technology giant Microsoft.

The motivation behind e-service market growth may initially have been self-serving for corporations, but the outcome has been positive for both enterprises and their customers. Service is increasingly viewed as the best differentiator between otherwise indistinguishable products and services. Companies have also reduced their servicing costs by deflecting customer transactions to the less expensive Internet channel. And customers who choose to use e-service are able to help themselves whenever they wish, thereby increasing their satisfaction and loyalty.

Consider e-service a common courtesy in the era of the Internet. Succeeding on the web today requires a strong e-service strategy that compels customers to select this less expensive servicing channel. Without solutions that allow customers to help themselves, an enterprise will create customer frustration, dismay, nasty calls and e-mails, and consequent servicing costs. To realize the greatest value from e-service investments, however, corporations must prioritize customer needs and wants over their own desire to reduce costs.

Designing a Compelling Web-Based Self-Service Environment

Customer service via the web is increasingly a differentiator for companies. It's obvious to web site visitors which companies have given thought to their customers' e-service needs and which appear not to want to be bothered by their customers (and there is a surprisingly large number of companies who fall into the latter category). Sites that offer compelling, easy-to-navigate, and easy-to-use e-service capabilities keep customers online longer than those that, by default, force their customers to abandon a web site in order to call to ask a question.

Building a compelling and friendly e-service environment requires analyzing and understanding your customers' needs—what information they want to be available online and how they want to interact with it. Long-term planning is required to lay the foundation for addressing current and future corporate service needs and then finding appropriate systems. (See Figure 5.1.)

Key Steps to Building the E-Service Environment

There are four primary steps in building an outstanding web self-service environment:

1. *Assess and prioritize customer needs.* Conduct an in-depth assessment of customer needs, and put customer requirements ahead of company requirements. Identifying customer needs may include interviewing and surveying customers, holding focus groups, examining existing web site usage patterns, and analyzing why customers drop out of the self-service system today. Once customer needs are documented, overlay your company's requirements and design a self-service strategy that satisfies both constituents.

Figure 5.1: Web Self-Service Planning Process

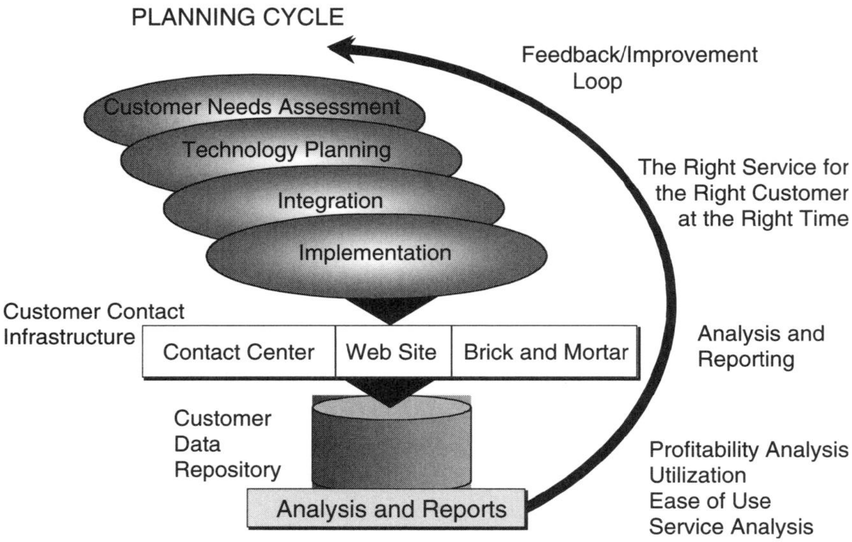

Source: Gartner.

2. *Identify technology and solutions.* Once all functional and system requirements are documented and the servicing strategy developed, identify
technology and solutions that will addresses current needs and can grow
with your company.
3. *Develop an integration strategy.* Integrating applications remains a challenge even as web services and other tools continue to improve. Ensuring that the selected applications can be integrated on a timely basis and
communicate effectively with the rest of the technical platform is essential for the success of your web site. Test out integrations before purchasing disparate applications.
4. *Implement.* After the testing is complete, implement the system.

These four steps are essential for building an effective and satisfying
web self-service environment. The ongoing challenge and most important success factor for maintaining a great site is establishing a continuous feedback and enhancement process that addresses changing customer
and internal needs.

Maintaining a Successful E-Service Environment

It's relatively easy to obtain support and funding to build new e-service functionality, but it's a great deal harder to get corporate support and funding to maintain the environment. Unfortunately, web site capabilities are often outdated the same year they are built, making web site maintenance a high-ticket item. In the era of the Internet, customer and company needs change quickly, and a site must remain current to keep customers coming back. When planning the project, the ROI analysis should include a substantial maintenance budget to ensure that the self-service environment will remain up to date.

Standard E-Service Modules

There are many standard e-service modules that can be bought and integrated into a company's operating environment. Some of these modules, including those for frequently asked questions (FAQ), chat, or e-mail response management are already perceived to be commodities. For other features, such as KM or workflow, there are significant differences among the various offerings.

The following are the typical e-service modules currently available. While some companies will use all of these tools (and more) to satisfy their customers' needs, most select only those relevant to their customer base.

1. *E-Mail Response Management System (ERMS).* Automates the handling of customer e-mails. A basic application manages e-mail flow in and out of an organization and uses key words to route and queue transactions. An advanced ERMS uses natural language processing (NLP) to identify and understand the content and intents contained in an e-mail transaction and uses this information for routing and to provide a fully automated response. At a minimum, an ERMS should come with the ability to automatically acknowledge receipt of incoming e-mails.
2. *Frequently Asked Questions (FAQ).* Enables customers to search for a specific question and answer.
3. *Web Self-Help (also known as web self-service).* Allows customers to look up information or log trouble tickets by themselves.

4. *Chat.* Enables customers and agents to type and send messages to each other while in a specific web site (similar in functionality to IM).

5. *Collaboration.* Allows customers and service agents to communicate interactively in a web environment (e.g., joint form filling).

6. *Universal Queue.* Functions as a funnel bringing together all transactions (web, e-mail, phone, chat, fax) into one queue. Once in queue, the program applies business rule workflow, routing, queuing, and reporting. The software allows organizations to standardize the handling of transactions regardless of channel of origin.

7. *Outbound E-Mail Campaign Management Software (CMS).* Enables organizations to issue e-mail campaigns and to receive and process the responses.

8. *vRep or Bot Software.* A form of self-service where the vRep or Bot takes on a personality, intended to humanize the interaction with the customer.

9. *Knowledge Management.* Allows customers (and possibly employees) to search a knowledge base to find the answer to a question. Knowledge management is often the underpinning of a web self-service offering. The more advanced KM environments offer sophisticated authoring and administrative tools for creating and managing content. Another differentiator of both KM and web self-service applications is the technology used to facilitate the "look-up" or search. The most common, basic (and hated by customers) form of look-up is "key word search." It's difficult to use because success depends on the user inputting the right word to obtain the relevant answer. One step up is "key phrase search," where customers can type in a few words in the hope of finding the information they need. The most sophisticated web self-service and KM applications today are using "natural language search" capabilities that allow customers to enter a free-form sentence, such as "Please tell me everything about growing apples and, by the way, where is the best place to see apple trees?" The newer NLP-based KM and web self-service offerings are much better than previous solutions, but advancements in technology are still needed to improve accuracy and customer satisfaction.

10. *Workflow Software.* Provides an environment and development tools for automating work flows and processes. This software is intended to simplify operating environments and reduce the cost of servicing.

Selecting an E-Service Vendor

Once a company decides which applications and technology it needs, it's time to identify and select solution providers and business models. There are an estimated 50 vendors in the United States and abroad that sell e-service functionality, despite the fact that this market has consolidated and is expected to undergo further mergers and takeovers. Vendors fall into the following general categories, each providing different functionality, albeit with similar marketing messages:

1. Best-of-breed e-service suite providers
2. Best-of-breed point solutions
3. Contact center infrastructure providers
4. CRM suite providers
5. ERP providers
6. E-service ASPs

Best-of-Breed E-Service Suite Providers

These vendors generally offer at least four of the modules listed. The primary functionality found in e-service suites includes ERMS, chat, web self-service, and a universal queue that allows the e-service suite vendor to integrate its own channels, but not phone-based transactions. If a company wants to implement e-service functionality to improve quality, a suite makes a lot of sense. Vendors include eGain Communications Corporation, KANA, Inc., RightNow Technologies, Inc., and Talisma Corporation.

Best-of-Breed E-Service Point Solutions

Vendors of this type offer one or two of the e-service modules listed. While the breadth of functionality is limited, these modules may offer performance superior to that of a suite. The price of point solutions is generally more reasonable, as system users pay for exactly what they need, unlike a suite, where purchasers pay not only for the functionality that they want but also for other pre-packaged capabilities that, at best, they may need someday. The downside of many best-of-breed providers is financial instability and lack of viability. Vendors include Banter (acquired by iPhrase Technologies, Inc., in 2004) and NativeMinds (acquired by Verity, Inc., in March 2004).

Contact Center Infrastructure Providers

These are the old and new switching, ACD, and CTI vendors, including those that sell large switches and vendors that sell all-in-one solutions. Besides doing an outstanding job of handling phone calls, these vendors offer products that also manage data-based transactions such as e-mails and chat sessions, sometimes even providing FAQ. Infrastructure providers concentrate on managing the movement of transactions but generally do not go beyond key word-based routing. Customers who want advanced analysis and processing of e-mails, for example, must purchase and integrate an ERMS. Vendors include Aspect Communications Corporation, Avaya, Interactive Intelligence Inc., and Nortel Networks.

Customer Relationship Management Suite Providers

These vendors sell sales, marketing, customer service, and sometimes other functionality, like ERMS. Customer relationship management suite functionality has improved greatly during the past 3 years, and many of these vendors have much to offer to prospects, particularly for e-service. But this is a Catch-22 in that prospects are forced to invest in a great deal of functionality and infrastructure that they may not be ready for or even need. Vendors include Amdocs, Chordiant Software Inc., Onyx Software Corporation, and Siebel Systems, Inc.

Enterprise Resource Planning Providers

These are the classic ERP vendors that are building CRM and e-service functionality. This is an eclectic group, very different from each other but all lagging behind the leading e-service offerings in the market. They present a compelling message of integrated front- and back-office products, but while the three major players—Oracle, PeopleSoft Inc. (acquired by Oracle in 2005), and SAP AG—are all working to deliver strong e-service products, there is still much room for improvement.

E-Service Application Service Providers

These vendors rent or lease e-service functionality. When they first entered the market in 2000, many of the offerings were functionally inferior to the products available for sale. However, during the last couple of years, the surviving e-service vendors have developed solid products. Vendors include eAssist (acquired by Talimsa Corporation in 2004), eGain Communications Corporation, LivePerson, Inc., and RightNow Technologies, Inc.

E-Service Application Selection Guidelines

There are many functionally rich e-service applications and choices available, but the e-service marketplace is more volatile than most. Therefore, after identifying vendors that provide the required functionality, the first question to consider is vendor viability—that is, will the vendor be in business supporting and improving its application in 2 or 3 years? And does the vendor have the financial strength to invest adequately in new product development?

Second, it is important to assess the vendor's product strategy—is the vendor's strategic direction in line with your organization's current and future business needs? Does the vendor provide consulting and integration services, or are these functions performed by a third party? It's also important to find a vendor that understands your vertical requirements. Yes, e-service is a horizontal issue, affecting every business—profit and nonprofit, government agencies, and educational organizations—but how e-service is applied and determining the specific priorities varies by industry. There are an increasing number of vertical offerings and more are expected in the future. Finding a vendor with a good track record in your particular field or industry is critical for the success of the implementation.

The Selection Process: What to Consider Before You Buy

Choosing an application that is easy to implement and use on an ongoing basis is a must. There are systems that are expected to take a year or more to implement (such as enterprise resource planning), but e-service isn't one of them. A company should be able to successfully implement two or three e-service modules, such as an ERMS, web self-service, and chat, within 2 to 4 months. Of course, being able to implement quickly depends upon a company having a data repository available to support the ERMS library and the web self-service environment.

However, as the ongoing success of the e-service environment is only as good as the accuracy of the data used to feed the systems, it's just as critical to purchase a system with a response library or knowledge base that is easy to update. If you need the vendor's assistance to update your library of responses for any part of the system, it's unlikely that your system will be successful on an ongoing basis. In short, it's essential to go with an application that is easy to use, implement, and maintain and that fits into your existing systems environment without requiring a great deal of change.

Selecting the Vendor: Financial Viability

Once you find a couple of applications that meet your needs and are relatively easy to implement, use, and maintain, take a close look at the vendor's financials. Many vendors in the e-service marketplace are not financially strong. Even though e-service applications should not take long to implement, once installed they become an essential component of your contact center and servicing infrastructure and are not easy to pull out. It's important to assume that you are making a 5-year commitment, so selecting a vendor likely to be in business for the next 5 years is ideal. (Even stable vendors are at risk of being acquired, as in the case of Oracle's recent acquisition of PeopleSoft.)

Product Functionality: Buy Only What You Need

During the CRM craze at the end of the 1990s, enterprises bought a lot of software they didn't need and are probably never going to use. Some probably don't even remember that it's sitting on the shelf, and if and when they do, it may no longer meet their requirements. Vendors often offer substantial discounts for functionality or licenses that have no immediate use. Well, pass them up. Purchase only what you need, and build future purchasing discounts into your contract. Don't invest in software or extra licenses just because of a compelling price.

It is, however, prudent to purchase e-service software from a vendor that offers complementary modules that you are considering buying in the near future (within the next eighteen months). A vendor that offers multiple modules should provide a single administration and development environment to simplify management of the system. For example, if you are starting with web self-service but know that you are going to implement an ERMS within the next 18 months, it makes sense to find a vendor that sells both and offers a single knowledge base that is shared by both of these applications.

Integration: Worth the Challenge

Yes, you can implement most e-service modules without integrating them with your CRM and other enterprise servicing systems. However, the value of your e-service offerings increases exponentially, for both your customers and the enterprise, when they are integrated into your overall servicing infrastructure. Integration remains the most time-consuming challenge in the CRM world, but experience and open systems can minimize these challenges. Every e-service vendor will tell you that they are open, that they use web services, and that they are XML-enabled. This is good, but it still doesn't ensure a smooth integration.

The best indicator of an application's ease of integration is previous experience. If vendors tell you that they or their system's integration partner have done this particular integration multiple times, there is a good chance that they will know how to make it work in your environment. It's still prudent to speak to two to four integration references. If the vendor can't come up with references, the integrations probably didn't go as well as they'd like you to believe or weren't done at all. In either case, your prospective integration initiative is at risk.

Best-of-breed Versus Suite

Neither best-of-breed nor suite is definitively the better choice; the best answer is dynamic, based on the needs of your company and the opportunities in the market. There have been periods of greater than 1 year when only best-of-breed vendors sold a specific application functionality that gave a company a competitive advantage, as was the case with ERMS. It took almost 3 years before CRM and ERP suite vendors adopted this functionality, and in many cases what suite vendors sell is still inferior to the dedicated e-service offerings. Many multi-function suite vendors continue to scare prospects with the specter of the "integration challenge." They are right that it's easier to go with a fully integrated suite of products, but you have to weigh your options carefully, keeping in mind that there are costs associated with both complex integration and gaps in functionality. If a particular functionality in a suite isn't available or is inferior to the offering of a point solution provider, then the organization should conduct an ROI analysis to determine which product offers the greatest benefit.

Hosting Versus Purchase

As recently as 2000, e-service ASPs or hosting companies didn't have a great deal to offer and much of what they did make available was functionally inferior to the offerings of product vendors. Now, however, there are many functionally rich e-service vendors that offer their products for sale or for rent, and the surviving "rent-only" e-service hosting companies have improved their solutions. The decision either to purchase or to rent (host) is often driven by budgetary constraints—whether an organization has capital funds or just access to an operating budget. It's unfortunate that important software decisions are being driven by companies' artificial budget limitations. If an application is going to be used for more than 3 years, it makes more sense in most cases to purchase. Organizations that host to avoid a large up-front capital expenditure may not be making the optimal long-term decision. The good news for renters is that they are not compromising on functionality, and, in some cases, the accompanying services justify the rental decision. As with many aspects of making the decision about e-service investments, conducting an ROI analysis of the buy-versus-lease options will determine the right course of action.

E-Mail Customer Service

E-mail is the second most common form of customer communication after the phone, and while it's not expected to exceed call volume in the next few years, it continues to experience a rapid growth rate. As a growing percentage of e-mails can be addressed with automation and do not require agent-based responses, companies should encourage customers to use this potentially less expensive mode of communication.

Automating E-Mail Responses with E-Mail Response Management Systems

Not all customer e-mails require human intervention. Enterprises should use an ERMS the same way they use an IVR system—to automate the basic and repetitive customer inquiries that represent 60 to 80 percent of a typical contact center's call volume, where agent input will not add value. An ERMS doesn't eliminate the need for customer service or sales agents, but a good application is able to analyze the writer's intent and tone, reducing the need to use people—who are much slower than a computer—for basic routing and categorization of incoming e-mails. Agents also benefit from not having to perform these boring and tedious tasks. Many of today's ERMSs also do a good job of standardizing and suggesting correct responses to incoming e-mails, allowing the system user to define an accuracy threshold and ensuring that responses match inquiries. Because ERMSs are not perfect, it's a good idea to set the accuracy threshold at 85 percent or higher, depending on each company's need to satisfy its customers. Using an ERMS to automate activities that don't require human beings allows an enterprise to use its most valuable resources, customer service or relationship agents, to respond to more complex inquiries that require the human touch and real cognitive thinking. An ERMS is recommended for any company that receives 200 or more e-mails per day.

Improving E-Mail Response Service Levels

Today, most customer calls are answered within four to six rings, but the typical 24-hour wait for an e-mail response to the same question is considered "good" service. Companies often send automated acknowledgments to customers who send e-mail inquiries. While it's better than nothing, those replies might as well say, "If your inquiry and time are important, call 888-888-8888." Too many enterprises still adhere to a 24-hour e-mail response goal, even though most executives surveyed indicated that they would never tolerate waiting that long for an answer if they e-mailed an inquiry to a company they did business with.

Most customers are reasonable and don't expect an e-mail response within 22 to 33 seconds, like phone inquiries. However, they're not willing to wait 24 hours to get basic information, such as the closest location of a movie theater, whether an online retailer has a certain item, or the name of a doctor. Why should they, when a call will yield the answer within minutes?

Depending on the urgency of an inquiry, 1 to 3 hours (not business hours, real hours, as the availability of e-mail outside of normal business hours is a great incentive for people to use it) is an acceptable response time and will attract customers to this channel. But even a 1-hour delay is unacceptable if, for example, a customer reports a gas leak via e-mail, something that has been known to happen. In that case, the response must come within minutes—in any case, one can only hope the person doesn't wait in his house for the reply! If, on the other hand, the customer asks the location of the nearest business office at which to pay a gas bill in person, the company may decide to take its time with a response; yet this time lag will likely delay payment and cost the company money. This underscores the benefits for both the customer and the company of being able to interpret the meaning and intent of each incoming e-mail so it can be prioritized and routed electronically. While the enabling technology, ERMS, isn't perfect, it's much better than condoning delays and wasting valuable resources—that is, agents—on this basic routing function.

Surveying to Ensure Customer Satisfaction

Enterprises that want to satisfy their customers should survey them to find out how long they are willing to wait for an e-mail response. However, this may disappoint some customers, as surveying creates the expectation that the enterprise is actually going to act on the interviewees' feedback. If your company surveys and doesn't deliver, customers will be more annoyed than if they had not been surveyed at all. Despite this risk, it's worth the effort to determine how long customers are willing to wait, on average, for an e-mail response. To manage customer expectations, it's a good idea to close the loop on the survey with a thank you e-mail that gives participants a summary of the survey's findings so they will believe your company is using their input and not just wasting their time.

Delaying E-Mail Responses Is Costly

The cost of delaying e-mail responses is much greater than most companies realize. Since a large percentage of customers will call if they don't receive an e-mail response on a timely basis, and because most companies (large and small) haven't yet integrated their phone and e-mail channels (54 percent according to a 2003 study by David Daniels, senior CRM analyst at Jupiter), organizations often respond to the same inquiry twice—first by phone and then by e-mail (even though the e-mail inquiry arrived first). Long after the phone call is handled, the customer may receive an e-mail response to the original inquiry. Making matters worse, sometimes the e-mail response differs from the response received on the phone, which causes the customer great consternation and can result in an expensive series of e-mails and phone calls as the customer tries to find out which of the answers is accurate.

These situations happen more often than most companies are willing to admit because their e-mail response libraries are not in sync with information used in phone service organizations. The failure to integrate phone and e-mail—the two most important customer communications channels—can increase the cost of a single e-mail inquiry (estimated to be about $6.98 by Gartner) to $100–$500. That's because the situation escalates from a customer simply asking an innocuous question to feeling compelled to correct wrong information through a series of lengthy service interactions. Besides wasting valuable resources and much time, the organization adds to the burden of customer service agents and creates a customer attrition risk—all because of a failure to respond to an e-mail inquiry on a timely basis.

Internet Security

Internet security is a top priority when considering e-service vendors. The unfortunate reality is that there is no foolproof method for guaranteeing the security of any web site. Some of the most secure sites around the world, from Microsoft to the CIA, are constantly being hacked. There is also a trade-off between security and ease of use. If your security measures are too onerous and obtrusive, customers won't use your site. Alternatively, if you don't have adequate security, you are putting your company and your customers' security and privacy at risk.

Most companies have extensive Internet security requirements and procedures. It's essential to make sure that any e-service product being considered adheres to your corporate Internet security requirements. If a solution does not comply with your corporate policy and the vendor cannot provide a quick fix, you should select a different application.

E-Service Return on Investment

All contact center investments, including those in e-service systems, need to demonstrate a quantifiable benefit and return within 6 to 12 months in order to get approved. Chief financial officers require hard dollar savings and cost avoidance as financial justifications for investing in an e-service application. Acceptable savings categories include productivity improvements, such as reduction in agent talk time or handle time, or cost avoidance, such as a reduction in call or e-mail volume to agents, or live sales visits. Of course, soft benefits, such as improvements in customer satisfaction, loyalty, and branding, also need to be considered when making a technology selection, but they shouldn't be used in an ROI calculation, as they are difficult to quantify and are unacceptable to CFOs.

E-Service Best Practices Implementation Checklist

E-service applications are essential, but if not accompanied by best practices will not achieve their goals. Consult this checklist to determine your progress toward building a successful e-service program. Adopt any best practices that you have not already implemented.

- ❏ Develop a flexible e-service/web self-service strategy.
- ❏ Prioritize customer needs over corporate requirements and ask customers what features and functionality they prefer.
- ❏ Ask customer service agents what features would most benefit their customers.
- ❏ Align customer and corporate e-service requirements.
- ❏ Build a feedback loop and continuously enhance the service environment.
- ❏ Plan on a large annual maintenance budget to guarantee that your site is current and compelling.

- ❏ Select a vendor business model (purchased or hosted) that provides your company with maximum flexibility.
- ❏ Carefully check the financial viability of all e-service vendors under consideration, regardless of their business model.
- ❏ Make sure the e-service module(s) can be easily integrated into your existing operating environment.
- ❏ Separate the e-service development effort into 6- to 9-month phases, each of which realizes a payback of less than 9 months.

6

The Strategic Role of Quality Management and Liability Recording

We are now in the era of CRM, an enterprise business strategy intended to improve corporate profitability by improving relationships with customers. Yet there is a widespread perception that service quality has gone from bad to worse. There is no question that companies struggling because of the poor economy do not invest a lot in customer service. During the past few years, cell phone providers, airlines, and ISPs were just a few of the groups that received negative attention in the press for poor customer service. It's likely that these companies view customer service as a cost rather than an opportunity to build a lasting and profitable relationship, which it is, when done right. While cost containment is understandable, poor service, which leads to customer attrition, bad press, negative brand image, and lost revenue, is not. Quality management helps companies successfully address the service challenge.

Recording systems, a fundamental component of quality management solutions, have increased in importance because of legislative developments. Recent laws, including the Health Insurance Portability and Accountability Act of 1996 (HIPAA) and the Federal Trade Commission's DNC legislation that went into effect on October 17, 2003 (and continues to be aggressively fought by the telemarketing industry), have compelled many companies to install loggers and others to seriously consider it. The DNC regulations for recording are complex, but the simple explanation is that any company that sells directly to consumers over the phone, including up-selling and cross-selling, must log 100 percent of calls. Even companies not directly affected by DNC should consider logging to protect themselves from frivolous lawsuits.

The Financial Benefits of Quality Management

Quality management applications were introduced in contact centers to improve service quality, but they didn't sell well until vendors marketed them for cost containment and productivity improvements. Quality management (QM) applications were developed to measure how well agents adhere to contact center departmental policies and procedures. They are used to identify agents who are not performing well so that they can be coached to improve how they treat customers and to reduce the amount of time spent on each call. This translates directly to a reduction in average talk time and significant productivity improvements for contact centers.

For example, if agents are not properly trained to handle a credit card charge back, they may waste 30 to 120 seconds asking unnecessary questions. This is aggravating to customers, and it adds unnecessary time to each call on the enterprise side. Once identified by a QM application, the specific agent(s) can be coached, the training program enhanced, and a quantifiable benefit realized by the contact center.

When quality management is institutionalized, the application yields benefits for both customers and the contact center and generally has a payback of 6 to 9 months. When companies use quality management to identify trends and revenue opportunities, an increasingly popular option, the payback will be even more rapid. Figure 6.1 shows the payback to be less than 1 month, whether quality management is used to realize only productivity improvements or both productivity and revenue enhancements. In this example, the ROI calculator assumes a typical contact center with 300 agents. The center handles 7.8 million calls per year with an average talk time of 180 seconds and an average work time of 45 seconds. The model further assumes that the contact center will realize the following standard categories of benefits from an investment in a QM/liability recording application:

- 5 percent reduction in call volume by resolving more calls during the first contact

Figure 6.1: The Quality Management ROI Calculator

Expenses

One-time investments			
Software license	$150,000		
Hardware	$50,000		
Implementation	$25,000		
Training on new system	$25,000		
Annual costs			
Software maintenance (18% of license)	$27,000		
Hardware maintenance (10%)	5,000		
Ongoing agent training	$50,000		
Annual call center savings			
Improvement in first-call resolution rate	$2,145,000		
Increased efficiency of managers	$15,000		
Increased efficiency of supervisors	$120,000		
Increased efficiency of QA specialists	$45,000		
Reduction in average call handle time (AHT)	$2,574,000		
Reduction in agent attrition	$30,000		
Annual revenue benefits of analytical oriented process improvements			
Reduction in inquiries from proactive problem resolution	$643,500		
Reduction in inquiries from providing feedback to marketing on campaigns	$429,000		
Increase in sales closure rate for marketing campaigns	$50,000		
Reduction in customer attrition rate	$1,500,000		
Reduction in fraud losses	$50,000		

		Benefits	
Total net benefits		Productivity	Prod. and Rev.
Projected Monthly Benefits		$403,083	$625,792
Projected Annualized Benefits		$4,837,000	$7,509,500
Return on investment			
Payback period (months)		0.6	0.4
Internal rate of return		1935%	3004%
Net present value (3 years @ 12%)		$11,367,658	$17,786,552

Source: DMG Consulting LLC.

- 6 percent reduction in average handle time (average handle time = average talk time + average work time)
- 2 percent reduction in agent attrition
- 1.5 percent reduction in call volume due to proactive problem resolution
- 1 percent reduction in call volume from providing feedback on marketing campaigns

The model assumes the following fully loaded salary rates:

- $75,000 per contact center manager
- $60,000 per contact center supervisor and QM specialist

As it generally takes 3 to 6 months for companies to become comfortable with a new application and realize the greatest benefit, it's advisable to add a few extra months to the payback estimates.

Overview of Quality Management/Liability Recording Market

In 1997, liability recording (or logging, as it is also known) and quality management were two distinct markets, each servicing contact centers. These two vendor groups started to consolidate their offerings in 1998, and as of 2003, all of the leading quality management vendors that did not already sell a 100 percent recording solution had added it. There are still vendors that do either quality management or liability recording, but most have given in to market demands for a complete suite of recording and quality management.

Quality management and recording solutions are increasingly viewed as commodities, because so many of the products have similar functionality. There continue to be differentiators in the product offerings, however, and new features and modules are added each year. The good news for prospects is that the solutions from all the top vendors and some of the smaller competitors are compelling. They are not functionally or technically identical, with major differences in a number of areas, including product support, product openness, product future, and company stability.

All the products will get the job done, as long as they are installed and integrated properly. Offerings from smaller vendors such as ASC telecom AG, Magnetic North Software Limited, Voice Print International, Inc., and Wygant Scientific may not be as feature-rich as those of the leading vendors, but they do deliver satisfying functionality.

Quality Management/Liability Recording Segments

Quality management/liability recording applications are generally considered add-ons to contact center infrastructure and platforms, so their market opportunity is often tied to contact center market share. While contact centers account for the largest component of the logging market, recording solutions are used in other businesses.

The quality management/liability recording market is divided into four primary segments:

1. *Public Safety.* Provides logging solutions for 911, 311, and other emergency services contact centers.
2. *Air Traffic Control.* Includes the Federal Aviation Administration and air traffic control.
3. *Financial Trading and Liability Recording.* Comprises total recording solutions for trading floors, brokers, sales, and any other organization that needs to be able to capture and replay calls for verification purposes.
4. *Quality Monitoring.* Offers logging and quality management solutions for inbound and outbound call and contact centers.

The market has tracked these four segments separately and will likely do so for years, as each has different needs, applications, and trends. The variations among the different segments of the recording solutions market are diminishing, as the underlying technology is increasingly the same. While it isn't yet viewed this way, these four sectors should be vertical offerings instead of separate product lines and markets. This would improve utilization of R&D investments.

Quality Management Product Capabilities

In the mature QM market, the majority of suites from vendors of all sizes include a standard set of features and complementary modules.

Standard Quality Management Suite Capabilities

Quality management solutions have evolved during the past 4 years, and the more complete suites generally include the following:

- 100 percent recording, advanced retrieval, and playback features
- Ability to record voice and screens simultaneously
- Capacity to handle multichannels—voice, e-mail, chat, collaboration

- CTI
- Software for evaluating and analyzing agent performance and trends
- Reporting (standard and ad hoc)
- Ability to maintain one copy of recorded calls
- API/software development tool kits (SDKs) to facilitate integration to CRM and other servicing applications
- TDM and IP recording capabilities
- A portal-based framework for delivering information to stakeholders (new in 2005)

Leading vendors have standardized on one technology platform, either Windows or Linux, for their product suite. When selecting a QM suite, it's essential to look beyond the product messaging coming from the vendors. Most of the products have the standard capabilities, but each works differently. Be sure the products you consider contain the specific functionality your center needs.

Complementary Modules

Quality management applications have been expanding to complement the core functionality of these suites, and QM vendors have recently started to offer these additional capabilities as part of their suites. The modules are also sold by stand-alone point solution vendors. These modules are:

- *e-Learning.* Learning management systems that author and deliver training programs based on the results of quality management evaluations or departmental needs.
- *e-Coaching.* Tools for rapidly creating and deploying coaching, communications, or best practices to agents.
- *Surveying.* IVR-based systems that survey customer satisfaction.
- *Performance Management.* Scorecards and dashboards that align the goals of a company with the objectives of its contact center. Scorecards can be developed for agents, teams, groups, centers, sales, marketing, and the executive suite.
- *Speech Analytics.* Word and phrase spotting, emotion detection, and content analysis applications designed to structure unstructured conversations so that customer insights can be captured and analyzed.

- *Analytics.* Online analytical processing (OLAP) capabilities that allow an organization to slice and dice data collected from the quality management and recording system, ACD, and CTI events.
- *Screen Auditing/Back Office.* Agent monitoring—initiated by an event on a screen, not by a phone call—of back-office functions.

The value of these new modules to contact centers has already been demonstrated. Nevertheless, companies should phase in these solutions, prioritizing those that offer the greatest payback.

Quality Management/Liability Recording Market

There are at least 30 players in the relatively mature worldwide quality management/liability recording market.

Leading vendors include Envision Telephony, Inc., etalk Corporation, Mercom Systems, Inc., NICE Systems, Verint Systems, and Witness Systems.

Smaller vendors include ASC telecom AG, Dictaphone Corporation, HigherGround, Inc., Magnetic North Software Limited, Magnasync Corporation, TantaComm, TISL, Voice Print International, Inc., VoiceLog LLC, and Wygant Scientific.

The majority of the revenues in the market, 65 percent in 2003, go to the top three vendors, NICE, Verint, and Witness. However, smaller vendors should not be automatically discounted, as they may bring innovation and more personal service to the market.

It remains difficult to accurately measure and compare the market share of the vendors in this market, as many of these companies report their financials differently. Because each vendor includes different market segments in its reported financial numbers, when making a selection, end users should ask vendors to provide the revenues for only a specific segment so that they can examine the vendor's commitment to that area of the QM recording market.

Market Consolidation and Expansion

A round of consolidations began in 2003, and more mergers and acquisitions are expected during the next few years. At the same time as vendors were buying each other, relatively new players appeared on the landscape, such as Magnetic North Software Limited in the United Kingdom and ASC telecom AG in Germany, to challenge more established vendors. The newest entrant, as of August 2004, was VoiceLog LLC, based in Gaithersburg, Maryland. VoiceLog was first to market in January 2004 with a hosted QM/recording offering.

New Product Areas

In 2003, the quality management/liability recording market expanded its product reach to complementary application areas, including e-learning, analytics, speech analytics, and performance management. Each is its own market with stand-alone vendors, but may grow quickly with the help of QM vendors who already have a large installed base to which they can up-sell.

Quality Management/Liability Recording Trends

Sales of quality management and liability recording solutions are expected to grow by 10–15 percent in 2005 and 2006. Sales of the newer applications, e-learning, analytics, speech analytics, and performance management, are expected to grow at an even faster rate. (See Figure 6.2.)

There are a number of trends driving change in the quality management/liability recording markets:

- *Migration of Contact Centers from Cost Centers to More Strategic Profit Centers.* As inbound contact centers become more actively involved in generating revenue, they will need to invest in recording solutions to conform with legislative requirements around the globe as well as to mine every customer interaction for additional revenue opportunities.
- *Legislation and Compliance.* These are increasingly serious concerns for companies. In North America, end users must comply with the 2004 Federal Trade Commission (FTC) guidelines, HIPAA regulations for insurance companies, and the Gramm-Leach-Biley Act (GLBA) for financial services companies. Outside of the United States, there are regulations in the United Kingdom for insurance companies, Basel II, which affects European banks, and regulations in many other countries.

Figure 6.2: Projected Growth Rate by Category for 2005–2006

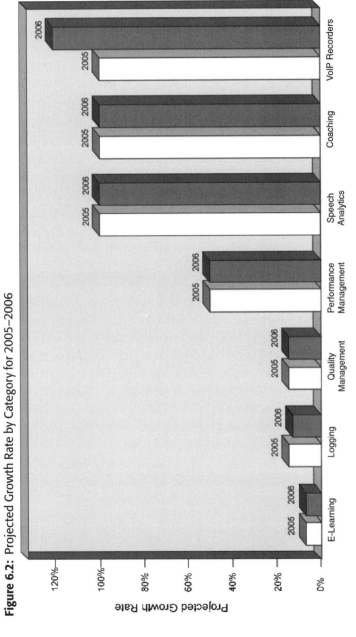

Source: DMG Consulting LLC.

- *Growth of VoIP Recording.* In 2004, for the first time the market saw strong demand for VoIP-based loggers in small and mid-size organizations. This growth is accompanying the adoption of IP-based private branch exchanges (PBXs) and contact center solutions. (A number of contact center infrastructure providers now offer IP-based logging solutions as a component of their contact center platform.)
- *Replacing Old and Outdated Logging Equipment.* Organizations are still using a great deal of outdated logging equipment that is no longer 100 percent dependable, a basic requirement for a recording system. In some situations, it's an analog solution that struggles to record digital calls, resulting in poor quality. In other cases, calls that appear to have been recorded can't be retrieved or replayed. While there are many reasons for the abundance of antiquated logging equipment in place today, organizations that have put off replacing it are likely to buy new logging equipment during the next couple of years.
- *Speech Analytics.* These new applications were considered a novelty through 2004, but enterprises are now considering the purchase of these solutions to help them structure contact center phone conversations so that they can identify customer insights, wants, and needs.
- *Coaching.* Larger and more expensive e-learning applications that include modules for formal training classes are still struggling for acceptance, but coaching has captured the attention of contact center managers, who see its value proposition and ROI as a tool for quickly and effectively communicating with their agents.
- *Commoditization of Logging/Recording.* Recording solutions are now considered commodities, which is putting downward pressure on costs, a typical pattern for commoditized products.
- *Professional Services.* The leading vendors are now offering professional services beyond system integration and are strongly encouraging their customers to use them.
- *Contact Center on Demand (CCOD) Offerings.* Outside of the United States, there are a quite a few network service providers (NSPs) selling hosted contact centers, which also include recording and basic quality management capabilities. (The CCOD concept is just being rolled out in the United States.) End-user organizations are increasingly logging calls for their own protection. However, the growing acceptance of CCOD offerings will shift logging and quality management revenue to contact center infrastructure providers and their NSP partners.

- *Shift from Hardware-Based to Software-Oriented Recording Solutions.* End-user organizations are increasingly seeking software-based recording offerings (in addition to quality management products that have always been software-based). The preference is driven by a number of factors, including the need to:
  1. More easily integrate contact center solutions with existing products.
  2. Share customer data with other parts of the organization, including sales and marketing.
  3. Reduce support requirements and TCO by using a standardized hardware platform.

Quality Management Best Practices

Automation and applications are essential for formalizing, standardizing, and institutionalizing QM programs, but these programs succeed only if they are accompanied by buy-in from contact center managers, supervisors, trainers, and agents. Quality management can rightfully be perceived by agents and supervisors alike as "big brother" applications intended to catch them doing something wrong. Whether we like it or not, quality management does play an important oversight role, although a well-designed program can accomplish a great deal more.

Contact center agents find it beneficial to receive accurate, targeted, and relevant feedback about their job performance. When employee performance evaluations are presented annually or semi-annually, as is the case in many companies, staff members are often surprised by what they see and are left to wonder why they weren't told earlier about areas requiring improvement. A well-developed QM program avoids this common problem by providing weekly or monthly input to agents. As agents can easily interact with more than 100 customers daily, timely and effective feedback (both positive and negative) is essential for agent performance as well as for customer satisfaction. Quality management, like liability recording, is therefore increasingly viewed as mission-critical in companies of all sizes.

Phone-based QM gives reviewers a lot of information about how agents represent the company, share product information, and adhere to policies and procedures. Adding the ability to simultaneously capture screen information vastly improves the effectiveness of the QM program and agent productivity. Watching how agents navigate their systems in addition to how they communicate with customers gives a more complete view of agent performance.

Here are best practices for building a successful quality management application:

1. *Make the system selection process inclusive.* Create a team that includes agents, supervisors, managers, trainers, and QM specialists to participate in the vendor selection process. Inviting agents to participate in the selection process gives them a sense of ownership.
2. *Draft agent evaluation forms.* Draft or modify an agent assessment that defines and evaluates the most relevant performance criteria. Be sure to also address section and question weights. Similarly to the system selection process, the team drafting the assessment should include all constituents and stakeholders, including agents, supervisors, managers, trainers, and QM specialists. It may also be a good idea to include a representative from human resources to assure that the evaluation adheres to internal requirements and to allow input from the QM process to be included in the semi-annual or annual evaluation process.
3. *Calibrate agent evaluation forms.* After developing the agent evaluation form, test it to be sure that it achieves its goals accurately and fairly. The testing should be done by a group that includes agents, supervisors, managers, trainers, and QM specialists. Continue to modify the form until it can be used consistently by all constituents who will be evaluating agents. Establish a process for reviewing the form on a quarterly basis to ensure that it remains relevant and is applied consistently.
4. *Train agent evaluators.* It's essential to train the staff members who will be evaluating agents. Calibration sessions will accustom staff members to using the evaluation form but won't teach them how to deliver both positive and negative feedback. The best QM programs are differentiated by outstanding coaching techniques.
5. *Define program parameters.* Decide how many calls and e-mails have to be evaluated on a weekly and monthly basis. High-volume contact centers typically evaluate 3 calls per month but can go as high as 20 calls per week in some shops. What is important is to select a number that is statistically relevant but not too burdensome for supervisors and quality management specialists. It's also critical to specify the number of coaching sessions evaluators must conduct per week. Coaching often

gets pushed aside as it is not always a pleasant activity and can be time consuming. For your QM program to succeed, coaches must be given goals, and one-on-one interactions must be prioritized. Some companies have started to use e-learning applications to provide timely input to agents, but there is no replacement for one-on-one coaching sessions.

6. *Establish program goals.* All constituents should be involved in defining the goals of the QM program and in deciding how this information is going to be reflected in the staff's semi-annual or annual evaluations.

7. *Define an exception process.* Agents need to have a defined process for challenging evaluations. Even in the best of circumstances and even when evaluations are correct, some agents will dispute their results. Build a standard exception process so that agents will feel that they have some ownership of the QM process.

8. *Set up the QM systems.* Once agent evaluation forms and performance parameters are defined, it's time to set up the QM program and institutionalize the process. For fairness, make sure that calls and e-mails are randomly selected.

9. *Communicate program objectives.* Before beginning the system selection, let your staff know that a new QM system is being selected and explain the goals of the program. Keep the staff informed on progress so that there are no surprises.

10. *Invite staff participation.* Invite interested staff members to participate in the different project phases. This will help ensure support for the process and prevent the staff from feeling imposed upon.

11. *Provide staff training.* While the majority of the newer QM applications are relatively easy to use, training is essential for successful implementation. Training should be addressed to administrators, who are responsible for creating evaluation forms and maintaining the system; managers, supervisors, training, and QM specialists, who are responsible for completing evaluations and coaching agents; and agents, who need to understand how the process works.

Building a successful QM program requires effort, planning, and internal selling. Sure, a QM system can be implemented, calls evaluated, agent assessments performed, and even coaching done without staff consensus. But if agents don't buy in, it will be a waste of time and, even worse, a negative experience resulting in agent dissatisfaction and attrition. Worst of all, it can lead to unpleasant customer experiences, as unhappy agents often convey their feelings to customers.

Keeping Quality Management Procedures Relevant and Up to Date

The vast majority of contact centers today have a formal or informal quality management program in place. Some contact centers do side-by-side monitoring, others use the ACD's service observe ports to listen to calls without agent knowledge, others use tape recorders, and some use QM systems. Whether you are installing your first formal QM system or upgrading to an enhanced release, it's a good idea to take a fresh look at your operating procedures to keep them up to date. Use the following checklist to review the relevancy of your QM program, whether formal or informal. As quality management is essential for the satisfaction of your agents and customers, for improving agent and supervisor productivity, and for keeping supervisors in touch with their agents' performance, it's essential to review all aspects of your quality management program every 9 to 12 months.

Quality Management Checklist

❏ Review your agent evaluation form(s) to ensure that the right criteria are being measured.

❏ Review the criteria weights on the form to be sure that the priorities of your company and customers are reflected properly.

❏ Modify the evaluation form and update the system, if applicable.

❏ Calibrate the evaluation form to be sure that it is still being used consistently throughout the contact center. The calibration should be done by agents, supervisors, managers, trainers, and QM specialists. Use the input to modify the form until it satisfies all constituents.

❏ Have all evaluators participate in an agent coaching refresher course. It can be as short as 1 hour, but it should be offered both to reinforce the importance of coaching and to answer any questions. Ideally, the course should include role playing where every-

(continues)

---

one takes a turn being an agent and then a turn being the evaluator, with a third person observing. After each session is complete, the evaluators should be given constructive feedback.

❑ Make sure that the proper number of calls and e-mails are being reviewed per agent on a weekly and monthly basis.

❑ Keep the lines of communication open between contact center supervisors, agent evaluators, and training so that information is shared on a timely basis.

❑ Review the training materials to make sure that they are relevant and in sync with current contact center priorities.

❑ Rotate which agents are being evaluated to ensure fairness.

❑ Review how calls or e-mails are being captured for evaluation so that the process is as random as possible.

7

The Role of Performance Management in Real-Time Contact Centers

Contact center performance management, also known as employee performance management, aligns corporate objectives with the tactical and strategic goals of all operating areas including sales, marketing, and customer service. Performance management broadens the focus of the contact center from strictly departmental goals to an enterprise-oriented set of objectives. It provides tools, processes, and a means for sharing time-sensitive, vital customer information with the rest of the company. It also offers automated data collection and reporting technology that frees up contact center managers to work toward achieving corporate goals. These enhancements in contact center operations are accompanied by improvements in agent productivity and satisfaction.

What Is Contact Center Performance Management?

Contact center performance management is a series of applications, tools, and practices designed to capture all customer interactions, analyze them to understand customer intents and insights, and then take actions to improve contact center quality and productivity as well as enterprise performance. Contact center performance management involves the use of a series of metrics to ensure that the contact center improves productivity *and* meets its departmental objectives, including achieving first-rate customer service, increasing sales, and enhancing customer loyalty. It accomplishes these goals by capturing, tracking, reporting, and consolidating a wide variety of contact center metrics. In a broader sense, contact center performance management converts departmental objectives into key performance indicators (KPIs) that are synchronized with corporate goals.

To ensure alignment with corporate objectives, contact centers must develop KPIs for agents, supervisors, and management. At the agent level, productivity measures should include average talk time and first contact resolution rates, quality evaluations from internal agent monitoring and customer satisfaction surveys, sales and revenue targets for new and existing customers, and customer retention goals. As valuable as each category of data is alone, when they are consolidated, analyzed, and applied on a timely basis, the result will be modifications in agent behavior that yield departmental performance improvements and also contribute to the overall goals of the corporation.

Figure 7.1 provides a graphic illustration of contact center performance management. Contact centers are the focal point of customer interactions

Figure 7.1: Contact Center Performance Management

Source: DMG Consulting LLC.

and, in turn, share their information with various departments throughout the corporation. As depicted in the figure, contact center performance management is the formal vehicle for transmitting this data on a timely basis.

Fundamental Functions of Performance Management

The basic functional components of performance management suites are:

1. *Scorecards*. Reports that focus on departmental goals and display performance at all levels—agents, groups, and departments (e.g., sales and marketing). For example, an agent scorecard will measure productivity, customer satisfaction, quality, schedule adherence, and sales performance (up-sell/cross-sell or new customers). A second set of scorecards will measure the success of a new sales campaign, such as analyzing which sales pitches are most effective, so that a company can respond quickly with the adjustments necessary to produce the highest sales. Comprehensive KPIs that reflect agent productivity, quality, sales, and stress levels are far more valuable than separate reports on various agent behaviors. For example, an agent may have been rewarded in the past for high productivity based on isolated information showing a low call duration and stress level, even though the result was actually poor service quality and customer dissatisfaction. Only when a wide variety of KPIs are consolidated with performance management can a company take appropriate action to modify agent behavior.

2. *Dashboards*. Customized measures of individual, group, or departmental performance, tailored to each user's needs. Dashboard displays enable an organization to take actions to optimize the customer experience, enhance the effectiveness of sales and marketing campaigns, and reduce operating costs. For example, a lackluster marketing campaign may cause more complaint calls from customers. As a result, agent stress levels spike. The marketing dashboard can detect patterns of increased customer frustration and agent stress related to the poor campaign. When abnormal stress levels are quickly detected, the marketing department can determine the root cause and take prompt corrective action. The contact center data are critical for transforming a marketing disaster into a successful campaign.

3. *Analytics*. A tool to slice and dice the entire spectrum of data into multi-dimensional components. For example, the performance management

application will capture data on agent talk time and number of sales. The contact center will measure how well agents adhere to departmental talk time goals. The sales department will examine the average duration of sales calls and correlate this with the data on completed sales. In the past, a high average talk time might have been seen as a negative. But if the resulting sales rate is high, yielding revenues greater than the cost of sales (i.e., average talk time), the longer call durations are actually positive, and agents who might have been penalized in the past will instead be rewarded.

4. *Reporting.* Flexible standards and ad hoc reporting capabilities that enable performance management systems to meet the needs of various stakeholders and constituents, all of whom want to see the data presented in a way that is tailored to their requirements.

5. *Action Engine.* A system that automatically identifies and assigns actions to optimize an opportunity or remedy a problem. Action engines detect agents who are outside normal operational parameters and advise supervisors to assign corrective programs. For example, patterns of excessive talk time and call transfers among new agents indicate a lack of product knowledge. Action engines identify and assign training courses, suggest opportunities to up-sell, and create effective marketing scripts. In effect, the action engine is an early warning system that quickly pinpoints negative trends, issues alerts, and advises remedial action.

The Benefits of Performance Management

The value of performance management solutions increases exponentially when the information that they capture is shared with relevant departments throughout a corporation. (See Figure 7.2.) Contact centers have sold products and services and solved customer problems for most of the past 30 years, but new performance management tools extend their value beyond departmental boundaries by making valuable customer information available for use by decision makers throughout the company. Contact centers specialize in identifying customer insights and needs, competitive trends, potentially harmful operational challenges, and customers who are about to close their accounts. Performance management provides the tools for encapsulating these time-sensitive customer data and translating them into actionable recommendations that can be passed along to corporate decision makers.

Figure 7.2: Benefits of Performance Management

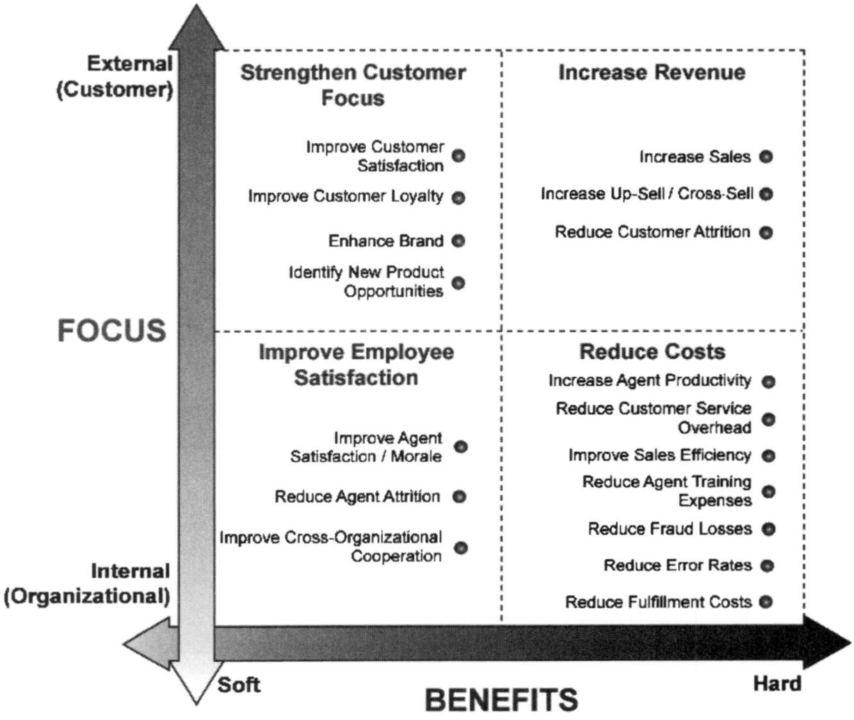

Source: DMG Consulting LLC.

Building a Successful Performance Management Program

To begin a successful performance management program, it is important to choose relevant metrics, determine what needs to be measured (KPIs), define goals, and decide who needs access to various categories of data. The next step is to select relevant feeder systems (ACD, IVR, CRM, workforce management [WFM], quality management, sales, KM, etc.) and then build the interfaces. (Today, as much as 25 percent to 50 percent of reporting adds no value to an organization. At the outset of a performance management initiative, take the time to determine which information is required before automating any existing reporting processes.)

Performance management is a solution that facilitates changes in people and process at the individual, departmental, and corporate levels,

Figure 7.3: Performance Management Components

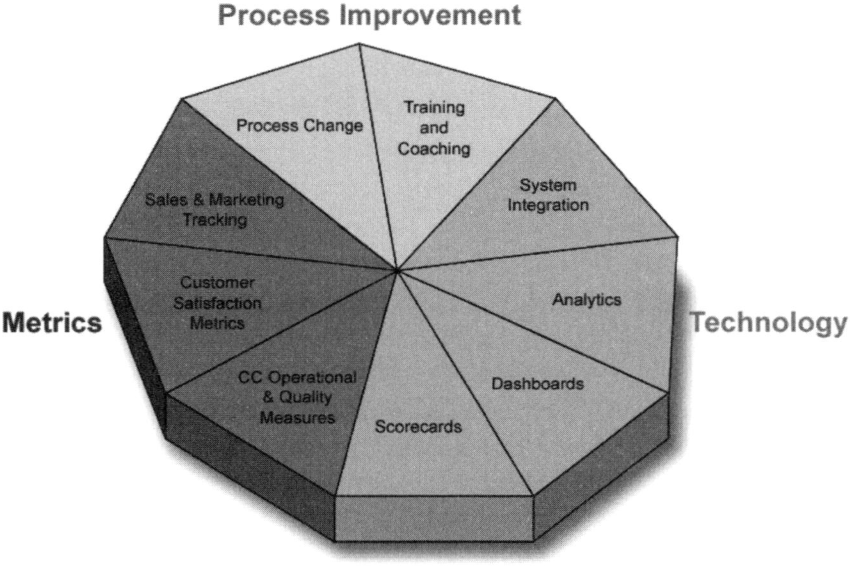

Process Improvement

Metrics · Technology

Source: DMG Consulting LLC.

but its success depends upon its being "institutionalized" as part of the corporate culture. (See Figure 7.3.) Enterprises that undertake a performance management initiative must be prepared to review and modify current systems, processes, and methods of delivering service and support to customers. Companies must be prepared to track issues to their root causes and expose all operating areas and functions, including sales, marketing, and other previously sacrosanct functions and policies, to in-depth analysis. As Figure 7.3 illustrates, there is a wide spectrum of corporate activities and functions that must be modified to achieve a successful program. This is a dynamic process that requires constant reevaluation and change.

Here are the primary steps that a contact center must take to create an effective performance management program:

1. Review the overall goals of the corporation and specific goals of sales, marketing, and other departments with which the contact center works closely.
2. Draft goals that allow the contact center to meet its own internal stan-

dards as well as the objectives of the corporation, sales, and marketing departments.

3. Define KPIs and other metrics needed to measure adherence to all goals, internal and external.
4. Identify sources of data for all KPIs and metrics needed to measure adherence to departmental and corporate objectives.
5. Identify systems that can provide the necessary data.
6. Determine existing system interfaces as well as those that need to be built to facilitate data capture.
7. Build required system integrations.
8. Design data warehouse file layouts that will be used for collection and storage of data.
9. Along with relevant external department(s) (e.g., CFO, sales, marketing), design report formats required to measure and analyze data.
10. Draft scorecards for measuring daily, weekly, and monthly adherence to corporate, departmental, and contact center goals and objectives.
11. Design dashboards for measuring adherence to corporate, departmental, and contact center goals and objectives.
12. Review existing reporting systems and reports to determine what can be incorporated into the performance management system and eliminate all redundant reporting.
13. Develop processes to reward outstanding achievement and correct substandard performance on a timely basis.
14. Implement cross-departmental procedures that allow the company to follow through on recommendations from the performance management process. Possible actions include improving sales tools, introducing marketing programs, implementing operational enhancements, and improving training and coaching.
15. Integrate the contact center performance management process with the training and coaching function to ensure that both individual and systemic issues are quickly identified and fixed.

Winning Organizational Support for Performance Management

Corporations that have adopted a corporate performance management strategy are building processes to facilitate cross-departmental goal sharing. But if your company, like most, isn't there yet, the contact center should begin by reaching out to the executive suite, the office of the CFO, and other departments that it supports. It is important to gain an understanding of these departments' specific goals and objectives and to find out what the contact center can do to assist them. It will take time and a great deal of effort to successfully build interdepartmental bridges. It will also involve some convincing of colleagues in other departments, as many companies still relegate contact centers to back-office cost center status, even while acknowledging that they do a great job of selling and understanding customer behavior.

It will take time to build an effective contact center performance management strategy that addresses all aspects of the corporation. It's a good idea to start within the contact center and, after proving the internal benefits of performance management, work to extend its value to all relevant corporate constituents and stakeholders. (See Figure 7.4.) Once other departments see the quantifiable benefits of performance management within the contact center, they will be more likely to apply it to their own operating areas.

Figure 7.4: Contact Center Performance Management Cycle

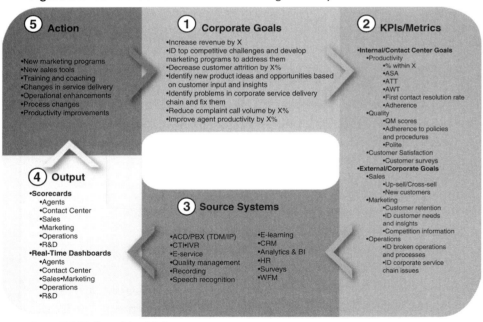

Source: DMG Consulting LLC.

Cross-Organizational Benefits

Performance management has a profound impact on how contact centers operate, measure their achievements, and interact with other departments in the company. It expands the contact center's focus from internal productivity and quality metrics to include objectives and performance measures that are aligned with corporate profitability goals. Performance management harvests and consolidates data from diverse systems to provide a comprehensive view of agents, customers, and the company's overall execution. Performance management systems require the cooperation of sales, marketing, finance, and operations in order to be successful. Along with new career opportunities, this also creates new political and organizational challenges for managers, who must learn to interact effectively with peers and senior management outside the contact center. Ultimately, everyone benefits: the contact center realizes improved productivity and quality, while the corporation enjoys increased revenue, increased profitability, and a more loyal customer base.

Business performance management yields benefits for customers, employees, and the corporation's bottom line by synchronizing the activities of all departments in a company. Performance management begins in the contact center, where a variety of KPIs are collected, analyzed, and synthesized to understand the impact of customer interactions and agent performance on departmental and corporate goals. Corporate decision makers have access to previously untapped resources—customer insights, trends, and behaviors. The consolidated data empower corporate decision makers to quickly identify the root causes of sales, marketing, and servicing challenges in order to take prompt corrective action. Performance management accomplishes all of this in a cost-effective manner, while decreasing expenses, increasing revenue, and enhancing customer loyalty and satisfaction.

Performance Management Market

The performance management market has been expanding since 2002. Some vendors have delivered generic business performance management applications that can be used by any company. There is also a group of performance management products that have been geared for use in contact centers, although all of these can be expanded for more general use as well.

To be successful, a performance management application must be easy to integrate, as it is dependent upon other systems for large volumes of input. Generic business performance management tools and contact center performance management applications have very different out-of-box integrations and scorecards. Applications geared for contact centers will have tools optimized to improve contact center performance.

Generic performance management vendors include Business Objects SA, Cognos Incorporated, Hyperion Solutions Corporation, Oracle, PeopleSoft, Inc. (acquired by Oracle in 2005), SAP AG, and SAS. Contact center performance management vendors include Aim Technology, Inc., Concerto Software, Inc. (acquired CenterForce Technologies), Merced Systems, Inc., NICE Systems, Opus Group Consulting, Performix Technologies, Inc., and Witness Systems.

Performance Management Readiness Checklist

Performance management will make valuable contributions to your corporation, but success requires a great deal of change within the contact center and the cooperation of external departments. This checklist will help you see how beneficial performance management will be for your environment.

Yes   No

❏   ❏   Do you have multiple sources/systems for the same KPIs and metrics?

❏   ❏   Do you receive reports with different results for the same KPIs? For example, do you get different average talk time numbers from your ACD and WFM systems?

❏   ❏   Do you have staff dedicated to reporting?

❏   ❏   Does your staff have to re-key data into consolidated reports?

❏   ❏   Do your managers spend more than 10 percent of their time manipulating numbers and reports to make them useful?

❏   ❏   Do your managers spend more than 70 percent of their time on internal departmental productivity and quality issues?

❏ ❏ Do your managers have to collect data from multiple systems, such as QM, ACD, WFM, and sales, to obtain a comprehensive view of agent performance?

❏ ❏ Do you create manual or ad hoc reports to show sales or marketing how well a campaign is going?

❏ ❏ Do you create ad hoc or manual reports to get a comprehensive view of agent activities, including contact center productivity, sales revenue, quality, and customer satisfaction?

❏ ❏ Would it benefit your company to have a system create automated scorecards for agents, the contact center, and other departments?

If you've answered Yes to six or more of these questions, it's time to seriously consider implementing a contact center performance management program.

8

Productivity and Quality Enhancement Systems in Real-Time Contact Centers

Real-time engaged contact centers require numerous management and supporting applications and systems to operate efficiently. Requirements for applications are driven by the contact center's business function, channels, size, purpose, and call direction.

Workforce management and e-learning are two management systems that, when used properly and consistently, improve agent productivity and service quality while reducing costs. Survey software, another management tool, is designed to measure customer satisfaction. Newer real-time survey products also help to reduce costs and improve quality by sharing survey results in near-real time with all operating areas.

Knowledge management is a supporting application that is generally used in contact centers that provide technical support to internal and/or external customers. Knowledge management (KM) applications promote collaboration and sharing of a company's data assets among its employees, partners, and customers. While challenging to implement, successful KM initiatives can yield a high and rapid ROI and huge improvements in customer and employee satisfaction.

Optimize Staffing: Workforce Management Applications

The basic purpose of contact center WFM software is to optimize staffing by accurately forecasting call volume and scheduling agents to handle the projected calls, at a specified service level. All contact centers that handle phone calls must use some form of WFM, whether manually with spreadsheets, or performed by a purchased application. Workforce management software is a requirement for contact centers with 50 agents or more. It should also be used in contact centers that receive more than 250 e-mails per day. Workforce management solutions also need to grow with an organization as its contact center expands to multiple locations and/or increases the range of supported channels. Managing agent costs while providing outstanding service is a fundamental but difficult challenge for all contact centers. When used properly and consistently, WFM software will help your contact center find the right balance.

Workforce management is the most maligned application in contact centers, and as recently as 1999 it deserved this reputation. The basic mathematical algorithms for forecasting telephone line and agent requirements are still based on the original Erlang calculations. But WFM solutions are now easier to use, handle skill-based routing, and address multiple sites and channels on technically open and standards-based platforms. The ROI from the newer crop of WFM applications averages 6 to 12 months.

Improve Agent Productivity and Customer Satisfaction with Workforce Management

Workforce management, primarily viewed as an agent productivity tool, is also essential for improving customer and agent satisfaction. Customers expect their inquiries to be resolved at the point of contact 80 to 95 percent of the time. To reach this goal, enterprises need to accurately forecast the total volume of transactions by channel, the number of agents needed to handle the projected volumes, and the skill sets required for these agents. They then need to develop and create schedules that match agents to projected calls. When this is done accurately, contact centers meet service level requirements and customers and management are satisfied. When there is a mismatch between projections and available agents, the service representatives are either bored and have nothing to do (something that doesn't happen very frequently) or they are overwhelmed by unexpected calls and e-mails and encouraged to speed up their handling of transactions. This results in rushed and stressed agents who often share their frustration with customers.

Reduce Agent Attrition with Workforce Management

To be successful, a WFM application must be accompanied by a WFM strategy that addresses agent needs. Contact centers are stressful work environments because the staff confronts the best and worst of society. Customers are demanding and not shy about sharing their opinions with agents. Agent attrition rates vary from less than 9 percent in the best-managed contact centers to more than 125 percent in "burn and churn" environments that care little for their employees. A common complaint in high-"churn" centers is changing schedules. Whether agents are full-time employees, part-timers, seniors, or students, few can change their schedules at will to meet ever-fluctuating volumes. Best practice is to use WFM to forecast and schedule, and then allow agents to select their own schedules. This practice works best if the WFM application is web based and agents, managers, and supervisors can access it from anywhere to reflect their schedule and vacation preferences. Agents can't control the inquiries they receive, but job satisfaction and willingness to stay put increase when agents are empowered to manage their own schedules.

Worst practice is forcing agents to bid for schedules and vacations. Agents are not going to change their personal and family schedules and vacation plans because their employer assigns them hours different from those they agreed to when they signed up for the job. It's fine to ask agents to shift their hours for a short period of time, if they are given adequate time to arrange their personal responsibilities. But companies that expect agents to arrange their personal lives around changing professional schedules always have high attrition rates.

Workforce Management Best Practices

Workforce management is essential for promoting agent satisfaction and improving productivity. Use the following best practices to build or enhance your WFM initiative:

1. Employ a mix of full-time and part-time agents to have flexibility for handling peak call periods.
2. Hire full-time employees for set schedules and do not ask them to change their hours, unless your company has absolutely no other options.

3. Hire part-time employees to meet peak call volume requirements. Do not require consistent overtime from staff.
4. Contact centers with highly variable schedules should hire a group of "flex" agents who are open to constantly changing schedules. Flex agents should receive a compensation "lift" to motivate them to fill irregular hours, just as an organization would pay a similar "lift" to the midnight to 8:00 a.m. shift.
5. Flex agents who previously agreed to schedule shifts should be given 6- to 8-week lead time, if possible.
6. Ask for volunteers who are willing to shift their schedules when call and e-mail arrival rates affect staffing requirements.
7. Minimize making short-term and frequent schedule changes, even for the part-timers and flex groups. The more consistent the schedule, the better your chances of retaining agents.
8. Reward agents for voluntarily adjusting their schedules by giving them first choice of vacation time.
9. If a contact center prioritizes work schedule selection based on seniority, vacation options should be based on the same criterion. However, seniority is not the best method for assigning schedules. This approach penalizes outstanding but relatively new hires. Contact centers should develop a system that takes into consideration overall job performance, QM scores, customer survey results, and other relevant performance measures so that the best performers are rewarded with first choice of schedules and vacation time.
10. Do not shift agents between channels without their consent and before providing the required training. Just because an agent is outstanding at handling phone calls doesn't mean that he or she can communicate effectively in writing. Some of the best agents quit when forced to shift to a different channel.

Selecting a Workforce Management Solution

There are a number of very good WFM solutions available. However, there is a great deal more to selecting a WFM vendor than just choosing a good product. These applications require an investment of 4 to 16 weeks just to get them into production. Prospects should select a vendor with strong domain expertise and a proven track record in helping its clients through a challenging implementation process. Here is a list of requirements to facilitate your vendor selection process:

- 6- to 12-month payback
- Ongoing vendor investment in relevant R&D
- Financial stability
- Strong management team
- Well-designed implementation process and training
- A reputation for providing great client support

Standard WFM functionality includes web-based system administration and agent participation, ability for agents to manage their own schedules, multisite capabilities, accommodation of skill-based routing, customer segmentation and other sophisticated routing requirements, multiple channel functionality, agent adherence reporting, advanced "what if" capabilities, planning and costing, standard reporting, and ad hoc reporting. Because the leading WFM vendors offer suites with such similar functionality, selection is often based on other criteria, including experience of implementation team, knowledge of contact center infrastructure, knowledge of WFM best practices, and willingness to share expertise without charging extra for consulting beyond the cost of the implementation.

Many contact center vendors, including those selling contact center infrastructure, WFM, QM, e-learning, and surveying solutions, are trying to increase their revenues by building consulting practices. This trend began in 2003 and is expected to continue through 2007. Be sure that you get the services your company pays for. Some of these vendors are repackaging basic implementation services under a new pricing category called professional services. Others are selling value-added services that will enhance your operating environment. If you see "professional services" in the pricing in addition to an implementation charge, ask what you are getting for the extra expense.

The Workforce Management Market

While there has been growth in the WFM market during the past few years, the top three vendors (Aspect, IEX, and Blue Pumpkin, which was acquired by Witness Systems in 2005) account for two-thirds of the license revenues in 2003 (according to the Frost and Sullivan 2003 World Agent Performance Optimization Markets). Genesys Telecommunications Laboratories Inc. is an up-and-comer in this market and, as a subsidiary of France-based Alcatel, has the advantage of substantial international distribution channels. Vendors include Aspect, Blue Pumpkin (acquired by Witness Systems in 2005), CenterForce Technologies (acquired by Concerto Software, Inc.), Envision Telephony, Inc., Genesys Telecommunications Laboratories, Inc., Global Management Technologies Corp. (GMT), IEX Corporation, ISC Consultants, Inc., Left Bank Solutions Inc., OdySoft Inc., Pipkins, Inc., Portage Communications, Inc., and Symon Communications Inc. Through 2004, the majority of the WFM product offerings were designed for United States–based contact centers with more than 100 agents. The market sweet spot was contact centers with 250-plus agents. By mid-2005, expect to see more feature-rich offerings directed at small and mid-size contact centers.

Surveying Software

Surveying software has had a hard time breaking into contact centers because it had the fatal flaw of not paying for itself with hard-dollar savings in less than 1 year. Chief financial officers are not paid to care what customers think about their company and are generally inclined to approve only investments with a quantifiable payback. The great news is that there is a new breed of actionable real-time surveying solutions being introduced to the market. These systems include traditional surveying functionality that allows companies to create and issue surveys in a number of channels, including mail, web, e-mail, and phone. They also include the tools to collect and analyze the responses and report the findings. Where these products break with the past is in what happens to the data once it is analyzed. The new real-time survey systems are designed to be actionable and bring about immediate change. For example, if customers communicate dissatisfaction with a specific corporate policy, this will be shared with the relevant operating area and the policy can be changed on a timely basis, before upsetting more customers. In the past, surveys were conducted and data collected, but by the time anything was done with the information, it was often too late to prevent the problem from affecting many customers.

The Value Proposition for Surveying Software

Even though surveying applications can be hard to cost justify, they are critical to the success of an enterprise and its contact center(s), as they convey customer satisfaction and dissatisfaction, which correlates to the lifetime value of your customer. The only way to know if a customer is loyal and willing to buy more from your company is to ask him or her. And a survey, whether conducted by phone, IVR, e-mail, web, or mail, is the most convenient and cost effective way to find out. A company's best prospects are often its existing customers, and surveying software is essential for understanding their needs.

The importance of surveying software is growing as enterprises shift from using reactive research-gathering devices to feed a data warehouse or data mart to real-time systems geared to engaging customers and prospects by providing a sales or service organization with immediate insights and opportunities. A survey is a great communication device and should be used to let customers know that they are appreciated. The newer survey products enable near-real-time intervention and follow-up, which has been proven to be more satisfying to customers.

Real-Time Surveying Benefits

The surveying market has stayed true to its historical market research orientation until very recently. In 2003, a couple of surveying vendors realized there was an opportunity to take advantage of the real-time capabilities of their delivery channels—the web and IVR—which are both capable of obtaining, analyzing, and reporting customer information and acting on it immediately to enhance the customer experience and prevent small problems from becoming large ones. For example, one IVR-based survey system is designed to transfer unhappy customers back to a contact center supervisor so that their problem can be addressed before they hang up. This real-time intervention allows an enterprise to turn a bad experience into a positive one.

The majority of actionable surveying products respond in near-real time, close to the customer-initiated transaction. For example, some surveying products can issue a series of e-mail alerts or kick off a management analysis when a high-value customer closes an account. True, the customer wasn't prevented from closing the account, but he or she will be contacted within the hour to find out why, in the hopes of winning back that person's business.

Real-time surveying products can also be used to identify when customer satisfaction with a service or a product drops below a predefined threshold. In the past, this information became available only after hundreds, if not thousands, of customers were negatively affected. Now this information is readily accessible, and the underlying problem can be fixed within hours.

Evaluating and Selecting Surveying Tools

Surveying tools can be licensed, hosted, or outsourced—three viable alternatives. All forms of surveying tools allow for web-based development, and the surveys are predominantly delivered over two channels, the web and IVR. A large number of vendors offer both hosted (on-demand) and licensed offerings. And an increasing percentage of products allow customers to be surveyed in their channel of choice.

A number of large organizations do survey outsourcing, but none of these vendors provide real-time surveying. The real-time survey market is currently the domain of small and emerging vendors, many of which are not likely to thrive unless they are bought out by a larger player. The value proposition for surveying has increased as survey results have become actionable and integrated with operations, sales, and marketing organizations, so this market is now expected to grow faster than at any time in the past.

The three best-known surveying products used in contact centers are Customer Relationship Metrics, L.C., CustomerSat, Inc., and Satmetrix Systems Inc. Mindshare and Amae Software are two newer companies that are emerging with real-time surveying solutions and a strong appreciation of the importance of actionable results. However, there are many other web-based surveying tools that cost as little as $19.95 per month on a hosted basis or can be purchased for less than $500. Two vendors to look at are FIRM and SurveyMonkey.com. Interactive voice response–based surveying solutions are offered by a number of the quality management/liability recording vendors such as Envision Telephony, Inc., etalk Corporation, NICE Systems, and Wygant Scientific. ViewsCast Limited is another vendor that provides IVR-based surveying.

What to Look for in a Surveying Solution

End-user organizations need to prioritize their needs and decide which features are most important before beginning their selection process. Common surveying product features include the following core components:

1. Authoring tools
2. Issuing software (web, e-mail, and IVR)
3. Data collection environment (internal database and ability to integrate with external databases)
4. Assessment tools to collect and analyze survey results
5. Standard and custom reporting
6. Online analytical processing (OLAP)–based analytics tools for analyzing results and identifying opportunities

Characteristics to look for in a surveying application include ease of installation, use, management, and integration. The authoring environment must be simple and not require the skills of a programmer or senior business analyst. It must also include intelligence that prevents bias in questionnaires. The application must allow for rapid creation of multiple surveys, data collection and analysis, anonymity for respondents, and a customizable portal for delivering results to specific individuals or groups. From a technical perspective, the survey application must be open and non-proprietary, come with or integrate with a standard database (Microsoft SQL, Oracle, Sybase, IBM DB2, or Informix), use web services and XML for integration, and include application programming interfaces for integrating with common vendor platforms, such as Siebel Ssytems, Inc., PeopleSoft, Inc. (acquired by Oracle in 2005), or SAP AG.

As organizations shift toward a real-time operating culture, it's essential for the survey application to integrate easily with operating systems so that the results can be acted upon on a timely basis. Contact center agents must also be positioned to see survey results so that they can use the information to facilitate interactions with customers.

Surveying Best Practices

Use these best practices to optimize your surveying efforts. It's essential to obtain accurate information from your customers and to use the input on a timely basis.

1. Survey customers only when the results are going to be used to make a positive change within your organization.
2. Communicate survey findings on a timely basis to customers so they know that their time and input were valued.
3. Tie survey applications into operational systems.
4. Fix the problems identified by customers on a timely basis.
5. Survey customers as close to an event as possible. For example, survey immediately after they place a call to a contact center and before they hang up.
6. Invite and motivate customers to participate in surveys with incentives.
7. Keep real-time surveys succinct, with 3 to 5 questions, but no more than 10.
8. Conduct the survey in the customer's channel of choice.
9. Feed survey results into a data warehouse or data mart for future analysis.
10. Obtain buy-in for a real-time survey application from all stakeholders before making the investment.

E-Learning: Computer-Based Training

Contact centers strive to keep agents in their seats and maintain a high occupancy rate so that they are available to handle customer phone calls. A form of computer-based training (CBT) used in contact centers, known as e-learning, delivers training modules to agents at their desktops. The better e-learning applications can be integrated with the department's ACD via a CTI link, to the WFM application, and to the quality management system. E-learning is integrated with the WFM application so that the department manager can plan for and schedule training sessions. It's integrated with the ACD so that e-learning content can be pushed out to agents when call volume is low. And it's integrated to the QM application so that after the QM system identifies a training gap, it can notify the e-learning system to automatically assign the relevant course. For example, if an agent scores below a threshold in a certain skill area of a QM evaluation form, such as "greeting skills," the QM system will send a notification to the e-learning system that checks with the WFM system to see when the agent is scheduled for a training class and then launches the relevant training program.

A second e-learning application that started to catch on in 2004 is more of an e-coaching tool than a full-fledged e-learning system. E-coaching applications allow trainers or supervisors to rapidly develop and issue coaching materials. An example is a supervisor who, while doing quality monitoring, hears an agent do an outstanding job closing a sale. Using an e-coaching application, the supervisor can quickly create an e-coaching session that includes the agent's conversation and incorporates how screens were used. The supervisor can annotate the conversation and point out what makes the call so outstanding and send it out to other agents. With the new brand of e-coaching tools, this entire process can take less than 30 minutes to create. The value of the near-real-time feedback to agents can be huge and is measurable.

Cost-Effective Training with E-Learning

E-learning applications are a relatively new entrant in the contact center market and continue to struggle to capture a portion of the contact center's budget, even though contact center managers recognize the importance and value of these applications. The problem isn't in e-learning's value proposition, which is generally a 6- to 12-month payback. The issue is that contact centers have always been stingy about spending money on training, and e-learning is a training tool. It's important to know which agents adhere to departmental policies and procedures, and it's also essential to identify and retrain those who do not. E-learning applications are a cost-effective and timely method of training agents and should be a standard component in all contact centers.

Getting the Most from an E-Learning Program

E-learning is most valuable when combined and used in conjunction with a quality management program. The QM program identifies gaps in agent skills and best practices, and the e-learning application creates and delivers training and coaching to immediately address the problem. The more integrated the workflow between the two systems, the more seamless and timely is the delivery of the coaching and training. The most effective e-learning programs use a closed-loop process between the QM and the e-learning system. The process includes the following six steps:

1. Quality management identifies the skill gaps and automatically notifies the e-learning system.
2. E-learning system locates appropriate training module or facilitates authoring of a personalized coaching session (automatically or manually).
3. E-learning system delivers the appropriate training course.
4. E-learning system tracks and reports on success of e-learning session.
5. Agent success is reported back to QM system.
6. Quality management program reevaluates the agent on the retrained skills.

Although standard e-learning courses are valuable, the most effective programs are those that are personalized to address the individual needs of each agent. And as is the case for almost everything in the real-time engaged contact center, the greatest benefits accrue when the training and coaching are delivered in close proximity to the agent call.

E-Learning Best Practices

Here are a few e-learning best practices being implemented in contact centers:

1. The e-learning application must be integrated with the contact center's ACD, WFM, and QM applications.
2. E-learning systems must be technically easy to integrate with other contact center systems and infrastructure.
3. The e-learning system must take input from the QM process that identifies agent skill gaps.
4. E-learning systems must allow contact center managers and supervisory staff to quickly create and deliver personalized coaching and training to agents.
5. Effective training and coaching sessions should include snippets of the mishandled transactions and an explanation of proper techniques.
6. E-learning systems should allow agents to append their comments to a coaching session and return them to their supervisor or trainer.

7. The coaching session must be delivered on a timely basis, ideally within hours of capturing a mishandled transaction, while it is still fresh in an agent's mind.
8. E-learning should not be a replacement for live training, but complementary to it.

E-Learning Vendors

There are three categories of e-learning vendors serving the contact center market: content providers, learning management systems, and authoring systems.

Content Providers

Content providers can be further divided into three categories. The first group encompasses vendors whose products create interactive simulations of real calls. The second group of content providers teaches soft skills, such as communication. And the last group provides applications training to teach agents how to use specific systems within their shop. The e-learning market is filled with lots of small niche vendors that specialize in a particular industry. For example, one vendor may create content for the insurance industry, and another vendor may develop domain-specific training for health care companies. Content providers include Sivox Technologies Inc. (a simulation vendor), and Skillsoft PLC.

Learning Management Systems

Learning management systems (LMSs) are complete training systems intended to launch, track, and report how well agents retain information included in assigned e-learning programs. The systems should also be able to consolidate and use programs from various content providers, but this remains a weakness of many LMS offerings in the market. Despite claims that the solutions adhere to the two content standards, AICC (aviation industry computer-based training committee) and SCORM (sharable courseware object reference model), many LMSs are not yet able to use externally created content. As there is not yet a large library of independent contact center courseware, this limitation is not serious. However, as new courses are delivered to the market during the next few years and e-learning is adopted in more contact centers, end users are going to pressure vendors to accept content that adheres to these two standards. Dictaphone Corporation, Knowlagent, and Witness Systems are the three primary providers of LMSs to the contact center market.

Authoring Systems

Contact centers use authoring systems to produce training materials and programs for agents. These applications can import data from external environments, including Word, web sites, and knowledge bases. Authoring systems format the data into computer-based training modules. These systems are available from LMS vendors, such as Knowlagent and Witness Systems, and from specialty vendors, such as Quarbon.

Implementing a Knowledge Management Program

Knowledge management is both an enterprise strategy and a software solution. But companies that implement a KM application without first addressing their existing strategy and corporate culture will likely fail to realize the projected benefits and ROI. A successful KM implementation depends 80 percent upon cultural change and 20 percent upon the technology.

Despite the organizational challenges in implementing KM, it delivers great benefits for three types of contact centers:

1. Those handling complex products and services
2. Those dealing with high volumes of transactions with high agent turnover
3. Those providing web-based self-service

The appeal of KM can be explained by its very high ROI and the improvements in quality and customer satisfaction that it produces. This is a technology with a very high risk/reward rating. The risk of failure is as high as 80 percent for contact centers, but the return and corporate benefits are even higher, generally millions of dollars annually for companies that succeed.

Common Uses of Knowledge Management Applications

Knowledge management applications provide a technology infrastructure for organizations to author, store, organize, access, and use information.

Knowledge management systems are basically intended to be large reserves of relevant information that agents can easily access to address customer inquiries. The products are designed to facilitate collaboration and information sharing between agents and other departments. They are invaluable in all contact centers that support complex products and services, as they can retain an unlimited amount of information, which human beings cannot. Knowledge management is ideal for help desks that service high- and low-tech consumer products (like cell phones and refrigerators), as they standardize the information agents provide to customers. Knowledge management is also an asset in health care and pharmaceutical contact centers, where providing the right answer could mean the difference between life and death. Of course, KM systems achieve their desired results only if an agent takes the time to look up answers in the knowledge base.

To date, web self-service is the most successful use of KM technology. An increasing percentage of companies have embedded a rudimentary or advanced KM application in their web site to enable customers to search for information and resolve inquiries without requiring human assistance. But the usefulness of these applications still depends upon human beings to keep the database current and consistent with information shared by live agents.

Benefits of Knowledge Management Applications

With use of best practices, a knowledge base that is up to date and timely, and consistency in all channels (agent knowledge base, web self-service, IVR, and partners), enterprises generally realize significant savings from KM applications. The savings come from the following categories:

1. Reduction in agent average talk time
2. Increase in single point-of-contact resolution rates that reduce the number of call backs
3. Fewer calls to more expensive Tier II and III agents
4. Decreased agent training time
5. Fewer inquiries to live agents
6. Empowered customers

These productivity benefits are great for the organization as well as its customers. Customer satisfaction generally greatly improves when KM is implemented successfully, as customers prefer to have their inquiries answered quickly and competently the first time they call. And, increasingly, customers want the option of helping themselves, even if they do not always choose to use the self-service channel.

Critical Functions and Benefits of Knowledge Management Systems

All KM systems have the following five standard elements and core components:

1. *Authoring.* Tools for creating and/or gathering content.
2. *Storing.* Open and flexible repository for storing content.
3. *Organizing.* Methodology for arranging information so that it can be retrieved easily.
4. *Accessing.* Enabling agents, customers, or partners to easily search for and find the information they need.
5. *Using.* Allowing agents, customers, and partners to easily use the information in the knowledge base.

Other essential functional components are:

- *Workflow.* Automating the review and approval of new knowledge.
- *Search Engines.* Text-based search technology for locating knowledge.
- *Natural Language Processing.* Use of semantic processing to attempt to "understand" the meaning of the requested search in order to improve accuracy.
- *Self-Learning.* An application that learns from prior searches by recognizing and identifying patterns to understand the cause and the resolution.
- *Self-Organizing.* Ranks knowledge in order of relative importance; knowledge that is less relevant will be ranked at the bottom of the list of information.
- *Support of Multiple Roles and Users.* As knowledge is used by different constituents, some internal and some external, it must be relevant for each user. For example, a customer service representative and an external user need to have knowledge delivered in different formats, but the core knowledge must be the same.

Two features differentiate KM from basic offerings and make them more valuable to users. They are:

1. *Portal Technology.* Personalizes the delivery of content.
2. *Structuring Text.* Captures and structures "unstructured" text in e-mails, surveys, web self-service, and other customer communications so that it can be converted to useful knowledge and categorized.

The biggest challenge remaining for KM systems is the need for people to create and maintain the knowledge base. Once this challenge is overcome, the time required to implement a KM system will drop precipitously, success rates will increase as dramatically, and the benefits and value of KM projects will grow. Of course, KM systems are useful only if organizations motivate their agents to create and access knowledge in the system.

Knowledge Management Marketplace

There are three main providers of KM applications:

1. *Customer Relationship Management and Customer Service and Support (CSS) Suite Vendors that Include Web Self-Help as a Component of Their Suites.* These vendors' products are perceived as less mature than those of the stand-alone providers and not yet functionally competitive, but are expected to improve over the next 3 years. These vendors are Chordiant Software Inc., Oracle, PeopleSoft, Inc. (acquired by Oracle in 2005), and Siebel Systems, Inc.
2. *Best-of-Breed KM Vendors, which Offer Feature-Rich and Mature KM Suites with Advanced Workflow, Authoring, Editing, and Publishing Capabilities.* These vendors are Primus Knowledge Solutions, Inc. (acquired by Art Technology Group [ATG] in 2004), and Knova Software, Inc. (formerly known as ServiceWare Technologies, Inc.)
3. *Web Self-Help Vendors and Hosting Companies.* These vendors' products are increasing in popularity because the applications are less expensive and easier to implement and use, even though they are not as feature rich as products from the best-of-breed KM providers. These vendors include eAssist (acquired by Talisma Corporation in 2004), eGain Communications, Inquira Inc., Iphrase Technologies, Inc. (which purchased Banter),

Kaidara Software, Inc., KANA Inc., Kanisa Inc. (acquired by Serviceware/Knova), KnowledgeBase Solutions, Inc., LivePerson, Inc., Primus Knowledge Solutions (acquired by ATG in 2004), RightNow Technologies, Inc., Talisma Corporation, and Verity, Inc. (which purchased NativeMinds).

Knowledge Management Best Practices

Companies must address both cultural change and systems to succeed with KM. Use the following list as a guide:

1. Accompany a KM system implementation with cultural change. This will likely require a complete business process re-engineering of the contact center.
2. Once a KM system is implemented, introduce rewards and penalties to motivate agents to use the system. Make the use of the system a corporate requirement.
3. Populate the knowledge base with up-to-date information and build a process to ensure that the data remain current. This will include a monthly or quarterly review of all information within the knowledge base.
4. Assign responsibility for knowledge creation and editing. It's fine to have a dedicated group responsible for creating knowledge or to allow all agents to author knowledge. However, no knowledge should be finalized within the system without a review to ensure accuracy and prevent redundancy.
5. Reward agents for authoring relevant knowledge.
6. Change contact center productivity measures to allow additional time for knowledge creation.
7. Involve contact center management, supervisors, and agents in the development of the KM system.
8. Make sure information provided by the self-service application is consistent with knowledge contained in the agent knowledge base.
9. Integrate the KM system with the CSS application.
10. Align the content in departmental training programs with the information in the KM system.
11. Train agents and knowledge engineers in the use of the system.

Cost-Justifying Contact Center Technology Investments

There are over 46 systems and applications that can be used in a typical contact center, as seen in Figure 3.2. When properly implemented, contact center technology investments yield a positive financial benefit to the organization and pay for themselves in 3 to 24 months—as contact center products without quantifiable benefits generally don't sell and fade from the market. Most of the systems can be cost-justified on a stand-alone basis. When the financial contributions of an individual system are not enough to cost-justify it on a stand-alone basis, combine it with a related system investment and justify them jointly. For example, include the cost for a survey system and/or process with an investment in either QM or performance management, as surveying is a key building block for the success of these applications.

The primary purpose of a contact center is to provide great service to customers, but few CFOs will approve investments in technology or people based upon quality improvements, which are considered "soft" and unquantifiable benefits. Therefore, the best approach for obtaining financial approval for a contact center investment is to justify it based on quantifiable hard-dollar contributions to the corporation. There are three categories that can be used:

- *Hard-Dollar Savings.* Agent or system cost is reduced as a result of a new system.
- *Cost Avoidance.* An incremental cost, such as adding agents, workstations, or lines, is prevented by implementing a new system.
- *Increased Revenue.* Revenue is increased as a result of a new system or process. (Chief financial officers consider incremental revenue only when a contact center is a profit center. Otherwise, the revenue is attributed to the sales organization.)

See Figure 8.1.

Figure 8.1: Contact Center Hard- and Soft-Dollar Savings

	Hard-Dollar Savings	Revenue Growth
Hard Savings/Benefits		
Productivity		
Reduction in staff	X	
Cost		
Reduction in calls	X	
Reduction in talk time		
(automated and agent calls)	X	
Reduction in hold time	X	
Reduction in fulfillment error rates	X	
Reduction in line charges	X	
Reduction in hiring and training		
costs	X	
Cost avoidance[a]		
Less hardware: ACD, PCs, phones,		
headsets	X	
Less software: licenses	X	
Less rent and occupancy: real estate,		
furniture, fixtures	X	
Revenue		
Increased sales		X
Increased profit		X
Decreased cost of sales	X	

	Soft-Dollar Savings	Soft-Dollar Benefits
Soft Savings/Benefits		
Savings		
Reduction in customer call-backs	X	
Reduction in abandoned calls	X	
Reduction in agent attrition	X	
Cost Avoidance[a]		
Less hardware: ACDs, PCs, phones,		
headsets	X	
Less software: licenses	X	
Less rent and occupancy: real estate,		
furniture, fixtures	X	
Benefits[b]		
Increased customer satisfaction		X
Increased customer loyalty		X
Increased revenue		X

a. Cost avoidance can be considered either a hard-dollar savings or a soft benefit. Enterprises looking to justify an investment should begin by consulting their company's technology investment guidelines to determine which savings and revenue categories are acceptable.
b. There are a few benefits categories that are real for the corporation but difficult for the contact center to capture and quantify, such as increased customer satisfaction, loyalty, and (possibly) revenue. As these benefits cannot be directly attributed to the contact center, they should be tracked but not included in an ROI analysis, as most CFOs will question their validity.
Source: DMG Consulting LLC.

Productivity and Quality Enhancement Systems Checklist

Use this checklist to determine which management and supporting systems will contribute most to the success of your operation by improving productivity, quality, and customer and agent satisfaction.

Is workforce management right for you?

Yes No

❏ ❏ Can you cost-justify the investment?

❏ ❏ Do you have more than 50 contact center agents?

❏ ❏ Are you using skill-based routing?

❏ ❏ Are you operating a multisite environment with more than 50 agents?

❏ ❏ Does your call volume vary greatly by day of the week, week within the month, and hour of the day?

Is real-time surveying right for you?

Yes No

❏ ❏ Can you cost-justify the investment?

❏ ❏ Does your organization value and use customer feedback?

❏ ❏ Are operations, sales, and marketing open to the input and willing to make changes on a timely basis?

❏ ❏ Can you change internal processes so that your company is positioned to respond in real or near-real time?

Is e-learning right for you?

Yes No

❏ ❏ Can you cost-justify the investment?

❏ ❏ Is training integrated with your QM function?

❏ ❏ Is consistently improving quality important to your organization?

❏ ❏ Will management, supervisors, and agents all buy into the application?

Is knowledge management right for you?

Yes No

❏ ❏ Can you can cost-justify the investment?

Yes   No

❏   ❏   Are you providing support for a technical or very complex product?

❏   ❏   Are you willing to change your culture and build a KM-oriented operating environment?

❏   ❏   Are you willing and able to invest in building and maintaining the knowledge base?

❏   ❏   Will agents, supervisors, and managers buy into the system?

❏   ❏   Do you want to encourage customers to use web-based self-service?

If you answered Yes to the majority of the questions for each section, the technology will benefit your organization and an investment deserves serious consideration.

9

Real-Time Analytics

Conquering the Unstructured Data Challenge

Contact centers waste 90 to 98 percent of actionable customer insights because they lack the process, technology, and applications to capture, analyze and leverage "unstructured" sources of customer communications, rich with information and feedback. Phone conversations are often recorded, but rarely analyzed for new revenue opportunities. The Internet opened online communication channels between customers and enterprises, but companies have struggled to exploit the unstructured customer data received over the Internet because existing data warehousing, business intelligence, and analytics systems understand only "structured" data. Customers, unaware of and unconcerned with these system limitations, freely share their needs and wants with contact centers and don't understand why the information they communicate is ignored.

Conquering the "unstructured" data challenge is the next frontier in contact centers and one that will distinguish proactive and engaged service and sales environments from those that are merely reactive. Enterprises that build a support infrastructure that allows them to immediately convert unstructured customer communications into actions—whether the information comes from a phone conversation, online survey, web form, web-based cancellation request, or e-mail—will have a distinct competitive advantage.

Real-Time Analytics Defined

Analytics is one of the most overused words in the technology market. Even worse, many of the supposed analytics offerings are really only reporting packages without OLAP capabilities—a fundamental component of any true analytics solution.

At the risk of defying prevailing wisdom, analytics is not reporting and not data warehousing, although it can use data from both these sources. Nor is analytics business intelligence (BI), decision support (DS), or personalization, although it may use these capabilities as well. Rather, analytics is a business strategy that uses enabling applications, including data warehousing, data marts, business intelligence, decision support, online analytical processing, modeling, personalization, and reporting to achieve its goals. (See Figure 9.1.)

Real-time analytics applications collect information from customer interactions, analyze customer data patterns and preferences in real or near-real time, and enable agents to take action, either while the customer is still on the phone or within 5 minutes to 24 hours. Real-time analytics applications are action oriented and include a transaction engine for initiating activities and a business rule engine that is seamlessly integrated with the transaction engine. Real-time analytics applications are capable

Figure 9.1: Analytics ≠ Real-Time Analytics

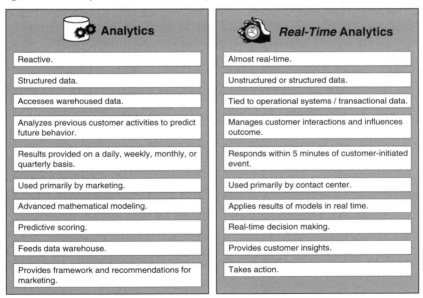

Analytics	Real-Time Analytics
Reactive.	Almost real-time.
Structured data.	Unstructured or structured data.
Accesses warehoused data.	Tied to operational systems / transactional data.
Analyzes previous customer activities to predict future behavior.	Manages customer interactions and influences outcome.
Results provided on a daily, weekly, monthly, or quarterly basis.	Responds within 5 minutes of customer-initiated event.
Used primarily by marketing.	Used primarily by contact center.
Advanced mathematical modeling.	Applies results of models in real time.
Predictive scoring.	Real-time decision making.
Feeds data warehouse.	Provides customer insights.
Provides framework and recommendations for marketing.	Takes action.

Source: DMG Consulting LLC.

of providing real-time decision support to facilitate immediate action. (See Figure 9.2.)

Figure 9.2: Real-Time Analytics

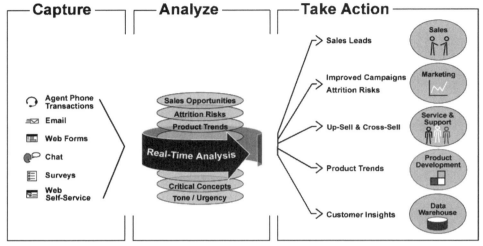

Source: DMG Consulting LLC.

Integrating Contact Centers into Corporate Strategy with Real-Time Analytics Applications

Real-time analytics is one of a new breed of technically sophisticated web services–oriented applications that are helping to share customer insights collected in the contact center with other operating areas. It does so by capturing and structuring customer transactions and identifying embedded insights and new opportunities. As the success rates in large-scale consumer campaigns continue to decrease and DNC legislation limits the use of outbound marketing campaigns, sales and marketing departments now have little choice but to ask customer service for help in reaching and selling to enterprise customers. During the past 30 years, the lack of cooperation and interaction between sales, marketing, and service departments has cost companies an unqualified fortune in lost revenue and opportunities. A major goal of the CRM movement was to get the three primary customer-facing organizations to work together, but this challenge remains unmet in the majority of enterprises.

Efforts are underway in many companies to open up the contact cen-

Figure 9.3: Agent Versus Real-Time Analytics Cost Comparison

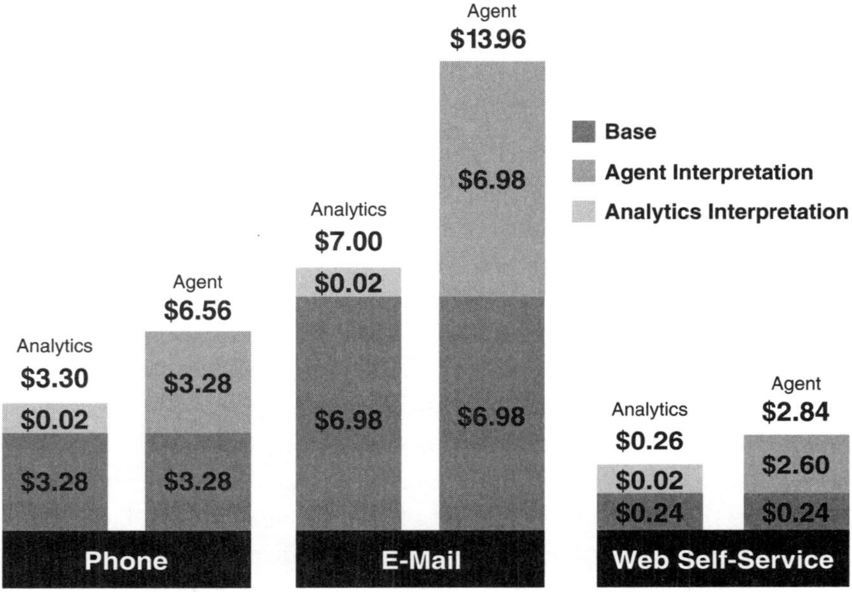

Source: Gartner, Inc., for the cost of a call, e-mail, and web self-service transaction.

ter, making customer interactions and feedback transparent to sales and marketing, so that all customer opportunities and insights can be exploited on a timely basis. The contact center is increasingly viewed as an excellent sales channel, but improved systems and best practices are needed to facilitate these efforts, as are improved cooperation and goal sharing with sales and marketing organizations.

While capitalizing on contact center capabilities is a corporate priority, using contact center personnel to translate and find opportunities hidden in customer communications is time consuming and doubles agent expenses. (See Figure 9.3.) As staff expenses already represent 70 to 80 percent of a contact center's cost, using agents to structure customer communications will eat away even further at potential financial gains. However, using a real-time analytics application adds only one to two cents per transaction, resulting in an immediate ROI of 1 to 3 months for most organizations.

Enterprises need timely, useful, and actionable information about their customers, and they need it at ever-increasing speeds. By converting large amounts of raw and unstructured data into useful information in a matter of minutes, real-time analytics gives an enterprise an advantage over competitors who continue to waste manpower and labor with unwieldy customer databases or even larger data warehouses.

Benefits of Real-Time Analytics

Contact center real-time analytics applications contribute to an enterprise's bottom line and to all customer-facing departments and operational areas, including the contact center, sales, marketing, technical support, and operations, as can be seen in Figure 9.4. Real-time analytics increases revenue and decreases the cost of sales when used to up-sell and cross-sell and to segment offerings based on customer value. These applications are used to decrease customer attrition and enhance brand loyalty by capturing and identifying the reasons why customers close their accounts and by uncovering customer opinions about competitors; by leveraging this information at point of contact, agents are able to counteroffer and retain customers instead of losing them and then working to win them back at a later time. Additionally, the highly valuable competitive intelligence can be analyzed to create proactive retention campaigns and/or to influence a product's features and pricing. Customers have always been willing to share their thoughts freely about products and service, but only recently, with the introduction of real-time analytics applications, have contact centers been positioned to use this information systematically.

Real-time analytics applications are used to improve service quality and customer satisfaction while reducing support costs by functioning as an early warning system for operational errors. Capturing information early on limits the damage, avoiding additional inquiry volume, production costs, and negative press. These applications are also empowering for customer service representatives as they can quickly qualify and quantify problems that previously generated large volumes of angry customer calls or e-mails. This results in reduced agent attrition. Lastly, real-time analytics increases first-call resolution, identifies training opportunities, and highlights new system requirements and fixes by quickly capturing and identifying system bugs. The products also add value by capturing customer recommendations for enhancements without requiring agents to write down all of the details.

Real-time analytics applications yield great results for individual

Figure 9.4: Corporate Benefits of Real-Time Analytics

Organization	Use	Benefits

Sales	**Enables:**
	
	■ Up-sell and cross-sell.
	■ Lead generation.
	■ Personalized selling.
	■ Identification of customer.
	  channel preferences.
		■ Increases revenue.
		■ Decreases the cost of sales by
		  providing more qualified leads and
		  identifying the most effective
		  sales channels.

Marketing	**Identifies:**
	
	■ Competitive opportunities and
	  challenges.
	■ Attrition risks and save
	  opportunities.
	■ Customer insights and new
	  product ideas.
	■ Market trends.
		■ Enhances customer loyalty.
		■ Reduces customer attrition.
		■ Allows development of more
		  competitive products.
		■ Facilitates personalized sales
		  campaigns.
		■ Creates better marketing
		  programs.

Customer Service	**Provides:**
	■ Customer feedback and insights.
	■ Recommendations for product.
	  and service enhancements.
	■ Timely awareness of operational
	  challenges that detract from
	  service quality.
	■ Identification of unhappy
	  customers who are attrition risks.
		■ Improves service quality and
		  customer satisfaction.
		■ Increases first-call resolution and
		  reduces callbacks.
		■ Decreases servicing costs.
		■ Identifies agent training needs
		  and reduces agent attrition.
		■ Detects systemic and operational
		  problems early on and reduces
		  their negative impact.
		■ Enhances public perception.
		■ Creates satisfied and loyal
		  customers.

Technical Support	**Supplies:**
	
	● Timely feedback on systems and
	  operational issues.
	● Detailed data for quality
	  assurance.
	● Ability to capture and identify
	  trends and problems.
		● Improves service quality and
		  perception.
		● Increases first-call resolution and
		  reduces callbacks.
		● Reduces expenses.
		● Identifies training opportunities.
		● Highlights new system and
		  process requirements.

Source: DMG Consulting LLC.

departments, but their value grows significantly when sales, marketing, and customer service share goals and objectives. Although these applications are designed to be used at point of contact, the results should be fed back into the corporate data warehouse for future analysis.

How Real-Time Analytics Works

The full power of real-time analytics applications can be realized only if new technology is accompanied by changes in operating procedures and training. The most prevalent use of real-time analytics applications in contact centers today is for up-sell and cross-sell. Many cross-sell applications are rudimentary and designed to offer the same script or reminder to all agents in either a specified group or the entire contact center. There are more advanced up-sell and cross-sell products that take a quick look at the customer's value, based on a set of predefined fields, and try to match offerings to customer needs. The more effective up-sell applications have intelligence to identify products and services that are most likely to satisfy a customer's needs, personalization abilities to adapt their offerings based on customer responses, and work flow for automating the fulfillment of orders. The better up-sell/cross-sell products are seamlessly integrated with servicing software. They must be integrated with the delivery system so that sales opportunities can be acted upon expeditiously. (It's critical to fulfill customer requests on a timely basis, within time frames communicated to the customer during the sale.) These products are more likely to yield positive results, although they are more expensive.

In addition to up-sell and cross-sell capabilities, real-time analytics applications can be a valuable organizational tool in a variety of ways. The following are some examples:

- Pharmaceutical companies can use real-time analytics applications to collect and analyze feedback from drug trials in order to meet federal reporting guidelines.
- Telecom providers concerned about retaining profitable customers should use real-time analytics to quickly identify at-risk customers and address competitive challenges before customers hang up and are lost to them.
- Financial services firms seeking to optimize the effectiveness of their marketing channels (print, web, e-mail, broadcast, and phone) can

quickly identify their most successful promotional medium and move marketing dollars accordingly.

- Retailers can rapidly assess customer satisfaction and capture customer recommendations to speed up product innovation and enhance their brand and customer loyalty.

Early Adopters Enjoy Great Results

As early as 2002, an online subscription business realized the power of real-time analytics for reducing customer attrition. When the company wanted to understand the reasons why its customers were canceling, it routed all account cancellation requests to a web site and asked customers to explain in writing why they were they were closing an account. Customers were open and generous about sharing their reasons, particularly when given a free-form environment in which to write their thoughts. Using an early entrant in the real-time analytics market, Island Data Corporation's Insight RT, the company was able to categorize the reasons accurately and enhance its marketing programs and products that reduced the volume of accounts closed.

In late 2004, an ISP that had outsourced its customer service function to numerous vendors with locations throughout the United States, Canada, India, and the Philippines wanted to be certain that its customers were receiving optimal service. Adhering to outsourcing best practices, it began surveying every caller to make sure that all problems were resolved, as well as to measure customer satisfaction and outsourcer performance.

A survey is launched after each call. It includes a tracking number that identifies the site and agent. The brief survey includes 5 structured questions and 1 unstructured question asking customers to share their thoughts on how to improve service. The company, recognizing the high value of the unstructured comments, tried to review all of the responses manually, but with a staff of five, they could address only 1,000 of the 20,000 responses received weekly.

Using Island Data Corporation's Insight RT, they were able to review all customer responses, ensuring that every customer received the necessary attention. The real-time analytics product has allowed the ISP to respond to 100 percent of customer requests for callbacks and to put in place procedures for identifying and resolving open inquiries.

From a tactical and bottom-line perspective, the real-time analytics application has reduced the customer churn rate by 10 percent and reduced the cost of retaining customers by more than 60 percent. From a strategic perspective, the real-time analytics product measures the performance of the different outsourcers by agent and location. It also produces reports for the various stakeholders in customer service, sales, marketing, product management, operations, and technical support. These departments can then use the customer verbatims and insights to improve their performance.

The Real-Time Analytics Market

The real-time analytics market is confusing, as there are vendors from many different functional areas offering "real-time" analytics solutions. Figure 9.5 reflects the variety of vendors claiming to offer real-time analytics. The majority of these products are not designed to capture unstructured text and phone conversations, analyze them, and take action in real or near-real time. Many of these applications are able to capture and analyze structured input, but only in a reactive mode, using old and often outdated information.

Real-time analytics applications are available from vendors large and small. Large vendors include Fair Isaacs (previously known as HNC), SAS, and SPSS. Small and mid-size vendors include Attensity Corporation, Blue Martini Software, Inc., InQuira, Inc., Intelliseek, Intelligent Results, Inc., Inxight Software, Inc., iPhrase Technologies, Inc. (which acquired Banter), Island Data Corporation, Sigma Dynamics Inc., and UNICA Corporation. The messaging coming from these vendors is similar, but the products are different. There is not yet a standard set of common features, as the market is new and evolving. The majority of these applications have been optimized for a particular purpose or vertical, such as analyzing content from customer surveys, e-mails, or phone conversations. This makes it essential for prospects to identify a solution that fits their particular needs.

While relatively new, a number of the products in this market are viable and have already made quantifiable contributions to early adopters. However, it's expected to take until 2008 for the underlying technologies used to structure customer communications to be more than 90 percent accurate in their understanding of unstructured text.

Figure 9.5: Real-Time Analytics Vendor Convergence

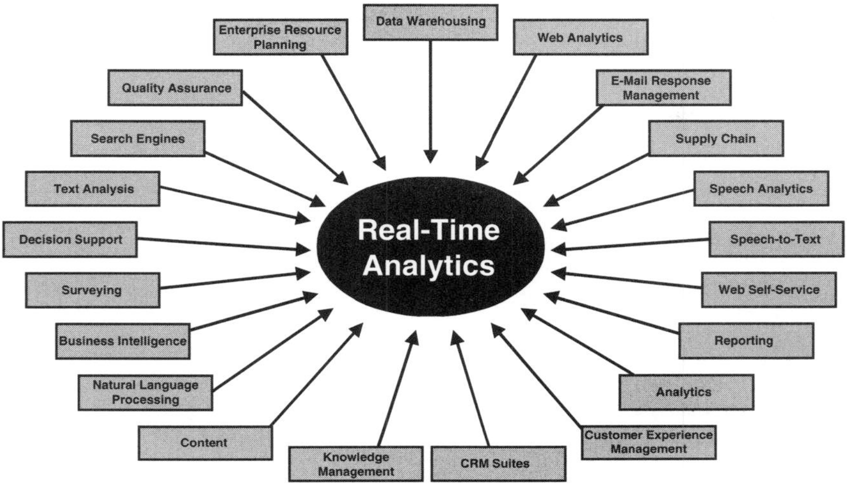

Source: DMG Consulting LLC.

Real-Time Analytics Best Practices

Best practices play an essential role in the success of any real-time analytics program, as contact center agents are often involved in offering or delivering the options identified by the applications. The best practices that follow will drive your success with real-time analytics.

1. Identify unstructured customer communications that include hidden revenue opportunities and customer insights.
2. Manually assess a small percentage of transactions to confirm the inclusion of revenue potential, customer insights, or whatever you are looking to identify.
3. Select a real-time analytics tool that is easy to use, can be implemented within 2 weeks, and is easy to integrate with existing systems.
4. Define key words, key phrases, natural language sentences, and concepts that identify opportunities and facilitate the analysis process.
5. Train the real-time application and enhance the definitions to improve data capture.
6. Manually verify the accuracy of training sets; once they are above the required accuracy threshold, put them in production.

7. Design new operating processes to handle output from real-time system within 5 minutes.
8. Obtain buy-in on new processes from sales, marketing, and service.
9. Establish new agent evaluation, compensation, and rewards programs.
10. Establish a feedback loop and enhance the system on an ongoing basis.

Real-Time Analytics Readiness Checklist

Within the next 5 years, more than 60 percent of large contact centers and 40 percent of small and mid-size contact centers will use real-time analytics systems to generate revenue, improve customer satisfaction, and reduce operating expenses. Use this checklist to determine if your company is ready to invest in a real-time analytics program.

Yes No

❑ ❑ Does your contact center currently provide, or is it gearing up to provide, proactive service and support?

❑ ❑ Does your contact center have goals and reward agents for resolving inquiries at point of contact?

❑ ❑ Does your company view its contact centers as a strategic tool?

❑ ❑ Is customer service viewed as a strategic differentiator for your company?

❑ ❑ Is your contact center responsible for generating revenue?

❑ ❑ Is your contact center a profit center?

❑ ❑ Does your contact center share revenue and marketing goals with the sales and marketing departments?

❑ ❑ Do your sales, marketing, and customer service organizations meet frequently to discuss common customer issues?

❑ ❑ Does your company measure customer satisfaction on a quarterly or semi-annual basis?

❑ ❑ Are managers in sales and marketing held accountable for customer satisfaction?

If you answered Yes to seven or more questions, your company is ready for real-time analytics. If you answered Yes to between four and six of these questions, then your company is almost ready, but still in need of change before realizing the maximum benefits. If you answered Yes three or fewer questions, then your company is not yet ready, but should revisit the issue in about a year.

10

Contact Center Staffing and Management

Contact centers are people-intensive organizations that require talented and dedicated staff, practical processes, and proven best practices to provide an outstanding customer experience while operating at optimal efficiency levels. To provide outstanding and differentiated service during every customer interaction, contact centers must invest heavily in their staff members' training and future. They must treat their employees the same way that they want the employees to handle their customers. Contact center agents who are treated with respect by management, properly motivated, adequately trained, empowered to take ownership of issues, and enabled with technology are positioned to delight customers.

Technology can provide needed information, but truly impressing customers in real time requires a combination of technology and the human touch that can be provided only by live agents. It is agents (also known as customer service representatives [CSRs], customer advocates, brokers, sales people, etc.) who either "wow" customers with great service or disappoint them with poor treatment. In an era when service is frequently perceived as the only difference between otherwise similar and commoditized products and services, the staff that touches customers directly drives customer perception.

Organizing and Staffing a Real-Time Contact Center

The success and market perception of every contact center and the company it represents are functions of its people. When customers complain about poor service, they are generally talking about people, not technology.

Figure 10.1: Contact Center Organizational Chart

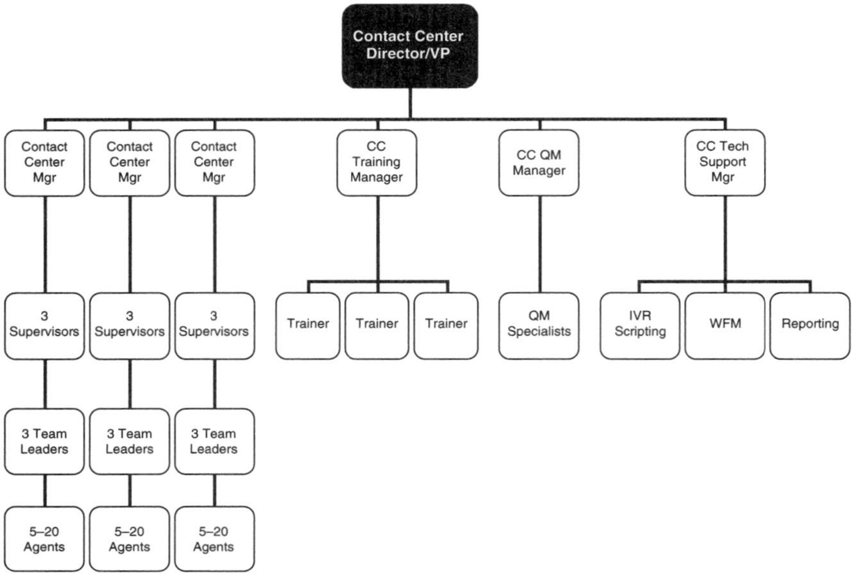

Source: DMG Consulting LLC.

One or two bad agents can hurt a company, as dissatisfied customers are very quick to share their negative experiences with others.

Contact centers require personnel with a variety of skill sets. To address the challenge of successfully staffing a contact center, enterprises must begin by defining the job functions they want performed and then draft detailed descriptions for each of these positions. The exact titles and roles will vary by company, but there are basic guidelines that apply to most contact centers. Figure 10.1 depicts a typical contact center.

It's a good idea to staff contact centers with a combination of full- and part-time agents, as this adds scheduling flexibility; it's recommended that contact centers employ a minimum of 15 percent part-time agents.

The ratios of managers to supervisors and supervisors to agents also vary widely from site to site and depend on the contact center's purpose. In shops that handle high-value or technically sophisticated products, the ratio of supervisors to agents may be as low as 1 to 5. By contrast, in a high-volume financial services call center where the typical call is "What is my balance?" the supervisor-to-agent ratio may vary from 1 to 10 to as high as 1 to 20. A ratio of 1 to 10 is optimal, as this will allow supervisors the time to get to know their staff and offer proper coaching and motivation. The agent-to-supervisor ratio also plays a role in agent attrition. A supervisor who is too rushed will not be able to devote the time required to help agents develop—an important component of every supervisor's job—which, in turn, will result in dissatisfied agents searching for a better work environment.

Manager-to-supervisor ratios also vary widely and depend upon many factors, including the contact center's budget. Typically, centers will have one manager for every two to five supervisors.

Contact centers are increasingly complex, multisite, and multifunction operating environments that require a new breed of leaders and managers. Contact center directors or vice presidents (VPs) should have direct management responsibility for the supporting functions that affect their job performance, including hiring, training, QM, WFM, and technical support. As contact centers migrate from reactive organizations to proactive and engaged operating environments, the supporting functions should be managed by a hands-on leader with day-to-day responsibility for agents, training, and technology.

Common Contact Center Job Descriptions

There are many different jobs and functions performed in contact centers. While the purpose of contact centers varies greatly—customer service, sales, collections, human resources, partner support, and consumer affairs—there are a number of standard positions found in most sites. Though the job titles may differ, the functions are relatively similar. In small and mid-size contact centers, some of these jobs are combined and performed by one person.

- Contact center director/VP: Manages the entire operating environment. Politically capable leader, as adept at handling service as sales and marketing functions. Must be technically savvy, analytical, financially knowledgeable, great with customers, and comfortable working with agents.
- Contact center manager: Line manager responsible for one to five supervisors. Responsible for the day-to-day operations of a team, including call/e-mail productivity and quality, agent scheduling and adherence, QM and customer satisfaction, and identifying agent training needs. Must be good with employees and comfortable speaking to customers.

- Quality management manager: Responsible for measuring and identifying trends and coaching agents to improve call, e-mail, and chat quality. Must work closely with contact center management, supervisors, and trainers.
- Workforce management manager: Responsible for forecasting and scheduling agents to ensure that the contact center is properly staffed. Must set daily schedules for all agents and schedule vacations, training, coaching sessions, and overtime.
- Technical support manager: Responsible for overseeing the applications, such as WFM, quality assurance, performance management, reporting, and possibly IVR scripting for the contact center. Reports either to the contact center director or to the technology group that supports the contact center.
- Contact center supervisor: Direct responsibility for managing a team of approximately 5 to 20 phone representatives. Duties include agent reviews, QM and coaching, assisting agents who need help with customers, and identifying agent training requirements.
- Contact center team leader (also known as contact center agent, level III): Second in command in a contact center team and most senior agent level. Generally handles calls that are escalated within a team. Assists supervisor and functions as an agent.
- Training manager: Responsible for working closely with contact center management, supervisors, and QM team to identify training needs and preparing and delivering training to ensure that agents provide the best service.
- Contact center agent, level II: Intermediate-level agent, with approximately 13 months to 2 years of experience. Able to handle the majority of calls without needing assistance.
- Contact center agent, level I: Most junior agent, generally with 12 to 18 months or less of experience.

Combating Agent Attrition: The Contact Center's Role in Career Development

The pyramid structure of contact centers—many agents, a small number of supervisors, and an even smaller number of managers—results in limited opportunities for agent growth and promotion. Outstanding agents can quickly rise from level I (entry level) to level III (team leaders), but beyond that, promotion opportunities are few. As a result, agents often view contact center positions as entry-level jobs from which to start their careers, possibly advancing in other departments of a company. This assessment is correct. Contact centers that accept their role as an entry point and work with their internal human resources organization to encourage agent advancement have lower agent attrition rates than those that attempt to prevent agents from moving to other jobs within the company.

Using the contact center as a career entry point can yield wonderful benefits to an organization. Contact centers generally have formal and thorough training programs that give employees a good understanding of the company's objectives. Also, contact center experience teaches employees to see things from the customer's perspective, which is often very different from the corporation's view. Seeding the company with employees who understand and are sympathetic to customer needs can only be positive for the overall goals of the corporation.

To retain agents, contact centers should encourage internal promotion, accompanied by external training to fill skill gaps. However, if skill requirements cannot be met internally, management should hire externally. Contact center management should always be on the lookout for outstanding talent and, once found, should motivate staff members with additional tasks and responsibilities. For example, an agent who communicates a strong interest in training and appears to have good training skills should be given an opportunity to work with the training staff to develop a new training program. There is always a need for innovation in training materials and programs, and giving a highly skilled agent the opportunity to make a contribution beyond his or her routine customer interaction tasks is a great way to encourage, reward, and retain the agent. Ideally, the contact center should have a 3- to 5-year management track that builds management, technical, financial, and sales skills in agents who display strengths in all areas required to manage the center. Further, contact centers should communicate all short- and long-term growth opportunities to internal and external candidates, to fight the perception that working in the contact center is a career dead end.

Hiring Best Practices

Contact centers require people with great interpersonal skills to assist customers, many of whom can be difficult. The hiring process is essential to the overall success of every contact center. Many best practices have evolved for staffing contact centers. Here is a list of commonly accepted practices that will improve your staffing success:

1. Hire people with an aptitude for the work that they will be performing. Do not hire someone for a contact center who does not enjoy working with people.
2. Define the ideal agent profile and detail the characteristics of people who meet that standard.
3. Match skill sets to jobs. An interviewee who has a great deal of patience and enjoys speaking to people may be well suited for customer service. An individual who is comfortable overcoming constant rejection is a good match for a sales position. Don't assume that just because a person is good with customer service he or she will be a good salesperson, and vice versa.
4. Do not assume that someone who speaks well will write well and move him or her from handling phone calls to handling e-mails without adequate training. Also apply this rule in the reverse situation.
5. Perform the initial job interview in the channel for which an agent is being hired. For example, if hiring telephone agents, interview them over the phone. If hiring e-mail agents, perform the initial interview via e-mail.
6. Give interviewees a chance to listen to simulated calls before offering them the job, to be sure job prospects know what they are getting themselves into.
7. Use a hiring skills assessment tool if recruiting a large number of staff on an ongoing basis.
8. Specify the shifts agents will be working *before* they are hired.
9. Provide agents with a detailed job description so that they are fully aware of the function(s) they are to perform.
10. Promote from within, whenever possible, even if additional training is required.
11. Be sure experienced contact center personnel conduct final interviews.

Training: Key Component of a Successful Contact Center

The only proven method for improving the quality of agent performance is training. Advance preparation and product knowledge are required for anyone to do a good job, but as contact center agents engage customers in real time they must be ready with product, system, and communications skills before taking any calls. Every agent contact results in a customer deciding to build, maintain, or end a relationship with a company.

Training Types and Methods

There are many types of training courses and many methods of delivering agent training, including classroom (with a trainer or via CBT), written communications, and e-learning (where training is delivered by CBT to the agent desktop). It's recommended that enterprises use all training methods, depending upon what needs to be communicated. For example, if a policy is being changed, an e-mail or pop-up will be sufficient, as long as it captures the agents' attention. However, if a new servicing system is being installed, the contact center will want to do classroom training. Here are a few of the standard training courses that are required for contact centers:

- *Basic/Introductory Training.* 2- to 5-week training program for new agents. The course teaches agents about the organization and its products and services. It conveys the company's service philosophy and instructs agents how to treat customers. The course explains contact center processes and procedures and how to look up information during a call with a customer. It explains how to get help and use departmental systems.
- *Advanced Communication Training.* 3-hour to 1-day course that instructs agents to improve customer satisfaction while efficiently handling a call, reducing average talk time. Agents are taught tricks, such as speaking techniques and better use of supporting systems. To be effective, this course must include practice sessions.
- *Up-Training.* Ongoing courses that introduce new products, present new techniques for handling existing inquiries, or review proper procedures for handling specific types of transactions.
- *Systems Training.* Explains the benefits of a new system or enhancement and shows agents how to use it to their advantage. (Contact center agents do not have the luxury of learning a new system by trial and error, as customers are not very tolerant.)
- *Account Retention Training.* 1- to 3-hour course that gives agents techniques and approaches for converting unhappy customers who are threatening to close their accounts into satisfied customers.

The Payback from Training

Agent training is a requirement, not an option, for contact centers. When done properly, training pays for itself and is a priority for companies that want to differentiate their service quality. It is very clear to customers which organizations invest in training and which ones do not. Customers do not want to waste their time with untrained agents, and when they reach someone who seems unskilled, they will often hang up and call back to get someone else. This cost is hard to measure, but it does add up.

Training expenses should represent 3 to 5 percent of the agent-related budget. To be effective, training must be ongoing. Proper training also plays an important role in agent satisfaction and retention, as customer service representatives do not enjoy disappointing customers.

Well-designed and well-implemented training programs generally pay for themselves within 3 months. It's one of the many contact center investment categories where there is a direct correlation between the investment and the return. For example, agents who have benefited from an advanced communications training course should experience a 15- to 30-second reduction in their average talk time. Agents who have completed an account retention training course should save 10 to 15 percent more customers than those who have not yet attended the course.

Evaluating the Performance of Contact Center Agents

Everyone wants to be evaluated and compensated fairly, including contact center agents. The frequency and consistency of agent evaluations affect agent satisfaction, performance, and attrition. Contact center agents are virtually tethered to the ACD and servicing system, such as the CRM suite, CSS application, or internal help desk application, so their every action is captured and measured. Contact centers that successfully retain their agents have developed thorough and fair evaluation processes that take into account agent productivity, quality, customer survey results, and sales numbers (if relevant). They provide frequent feedback to each agent on either a daily or weekly basis. A number of criteria used to evaluate agents are discussed below.

Annual and Semiannual Evaluations

It's essential to provide job feedback to all employees, including contact center agents and supervisors. The more frequent the feedback the better, but minimally contact center staff should receive a formal review once a year. The better operating environments will develop an annual or semiannual review that includes feedback directly from supervisors, QM scores, customer surveys, productivity measures, sales metrics, and attendance. To make the review a positive and motivating experience, contact center staff should be given an opportunity to respond to their reviews.

Quality Management Results

All contact centers monitor agent calls to determine if they adhere to the department's policies and procedures. An increasing percentage of contact centers simultaneously evaluate both agent calls and the screens used to service and/or sell to customers, as this provides a more complete view of agent performance and adherence to departmental standards. Most companies monitor 3 to 15 calls per agent per month; some use a quality management application for monitoring, and others either listen to taped calls or monitor live. Regardless of the method, it's essential to teach call reviewers to give constructive criticism and to provide both positive and negative feedback. Agents do want to know how to improve their performance, but they also like to hear when they are doing a good job. Providing consistent feedback to agents is a critical success factor in reducing agent attrition.

Productivity Measures

Contact centers continuously strive to improve agent productivity and must use quantifiable criteria to determine how effective their agents are. Standard productivity measures include agent talk time, wrap time, average call handle time, first-call resolution rate, average speed of answer (ASA), percent of calls answered within X seconds, percent of time agent is on calls, percent of time customers are on hold, percent of time agents are idle, percent of time agents are available, percent of time agents handle calls, total number of calls handled by agents, number of calls transferred, percent of calls handled, percent of calls abandoned, percent of calls handled by IVR, and percent of calls handled by web-based self-service.

Productivity measures are important, but they must be measured alongside agent quality, customer satisfaction, and revenue generation figures. It's wonderful if a contact center agent handles twice the volume of calls of the average representative, but if this agent's service quality is poor, the net result is actually negative for the contact center. To fairly evaluate agent performance and put each factor in relative perspective, contact center managers must take a holistic view of all aspects of agent performance, which can be accomplished with scorecards.

Customer Survey Results

The only way to determine if customers are satisfied with the service they receive from a contact center is to conduct a survey. The survey results should weigh heavily in agent evaluations, as they are the best indicator of service quality.

Contact Center Performance Management

This is the newest and most complete measurement for evaluating agent performance. Performance management applications collect, analyze, and report data from many contact center systems, including the ACD (for productivity), QM (for adherence to policies and procedures), surveying (for direct customer input), sales (for revenue), WFM (for schedule adherence), human resources (for schedules and salary data), e-learning (for training), CSS (for case tracking), and all other applications that are integrated into the contact center. For example, a performance management application will appropriately balance productivity, quality, sales results, and customer satisfaction ratings instead of forcing supervisors to look up all of this information and consolidate it into the agent's annual or semi-annual evaluation. A thorough contact center performance management program will provide daily and weekly feedback to agents, which is often greatly appreciated. Keep in mind that no one likes surprises, and the more immediate and well presented the feedback, the better the performance.

Managing Agent Attrition

Agent attrition rates vary from 5 to over 200 percent annually in contact centers. Attrition is a major contributor to agent-related expenses, albeit one whose cost is not often documented. The factors that cause high agent attrition rates are well understood, so they should be avoidable. Here is a list of do's and don'ts for managing contact center agents:

Don't	Do
Manage agents based solely on productivity measures, such as calls per hour and average talk and handle time.	Manage by performance statistics, but take a holistic approach that reviews agent productivity, quality, customer satisfaction, and revenue generation.
Manage agents based only on the subjective opinion of their supervisor.	Manage agents based on predefined performance measures.
Provide infrequent feedback on agent performance.	Provide daily and/or weekly feedback to agents so that they know what they need to do to provide outstanding service.
Yell at agents about large volumes of calls in queues so that they will rush customers.	Prioritize the importance of each and every call. Establish a process for eliminating nonphone tasks when call volume is high.
Embarrass agents publicly (in the middle of the contact center) about mishandling a phone call.	Have a dedicated private area for providing timely input to agents about their handling of transactions. Be sure to communicate what agents do right as often as they are coached on what they need to improve.
Take agents who are great at handling calls and assign them to e-mails or chat sessions, without asking them if they are comfortable in this channel.	Offer new opportunity to outstanding agents, particularly if it represents a raise and promotion. Be sure to accompany the new opportunity with training so that these agents have a good chance of excelling at their new jobs.
Frequently change agents' schedules.	Provide consistent schedules so that agents can plan their personal lives. Hire a group of agents who are open to constantly changing schedules, if there is a need.

(continues)

Don't	Do
Change agents' shifts from day to night.	Ask for volunteers to cover shifts. Since many contact centers pay a nighttime differential, there may be some staff who welcome this change. If agents do not volunteer, don't force them, as they may just quit; instead, hire new agents for this shift. (It's also possible to request short-term volunteers.)
Skimp on agent raises and give them infrequently and inconsistently.	Communicate time frames when raises will be given, based on job performance. Set expectations and then deliver consistently.
Hire new managers from outside the contact center or company, unless there are very specific skills that can't be trained.	Promote from within whenever possible. It's essential for agents to see that there is a career path and opportunities to succeed in your company, in and out of the contact center.

It's tough to be a contact center agent, as the public isn't always patient or pleasant to speak with. Since agents take a great deal of abuse, contact center working environments that are friendly, supportive, encouraging, and consistent retain agents longer than departments that are never satisfied with their agents' performance.

Successful contact centers with low agent attrition rates build a two-way relationship with their staff. Contact centers have a responsibility to define outstanding service and exactly what is expected from agents. They must also offer training, provide effective operating systems, and empower agents with tools so that they can do their jobs effectively. Most important, when agents need help, supervisors and managers must be available to assist them. Agents should not be forbidden to escalate inquiries and should not be required to take the blame for problem calls, an increasingly negative trend in contact centers. Additionally, customer service representatives should feel empowered to have a voice in corporate policies and procedures. Sure, they aren't going to be able to change everything they'd like, but they should be invited to provide input to senior management on improving customer satisfaction.

Universal Agents

Universal agents can handle inbound and outbound sales and service and can respond to phone calls, e-mails, and chat sessions equally well. Universal agents are ideal for real-time engaged contact centers, where representatives rarely know in advance what skills will be required for a call. During the next 10 years, expect to see an increasing population of universal agents.

People with the skills of a universal agent are desirable in and out of contact centers. They often make outstanding managers and salespeople, so contact centers are going to have to be innovative to attract and retain them. However, in seeking agents who are equally comfortable with telephone and written communications, keep in mind that although recent college graduates spend a lot of time IMing (instant messaging) each other and are very comfortable in that medium, this does not guarantee that they communicate effectively in writing, as IM has a language unto itself.

Determining Optimum Staff Size and Site Location

Managers need to decide the optimum head count for their contact centers. Similarly, they must also decide on the optimum number of sites. Given the flexibility of contact center infrastructure and, in particular, the benefits of IP, it's technically easy to have multiple physical contact center locations that logically function as one operating environment and deliver the benefits of one physical location. But there are decisions and trade-offs that must be made when deciding the staff size and number of locations for your contact center. Issues to consider include the following:

1. Are there business or public relations needs that require multiple physical locations? For example, a shipping company or bank may need to have storefronts in each service location that also function as part of the contact center servicing environment. While it would be more efficient to have one larger contact center than multiple locations with two to eight agents, customer needs drive the requirement.
2. Do you require international locations with locally based support staff that speaks the language and understands the culture?
3. Are there backup or contingency reasons for having multiple contact center locations? For example, if a hurricane were to close a location in Florida, does it make sense to have a second contact center on the East Coast?

Managing the Culture of Constant Improvement

Contact centers are dynamic, real-time environments that confront constant change and are driven by customer expectation, enterprise needs, and technological innovation. Some of these changes are small, and some will have a significant impact on the operating environment. Contact centers that want to maintain a competitive service edge must undergo a business process review every 18 to 36 months and make appropriate changes to people, process, and technology.

Contact centers that use manual processes and spreadsheets for WFM, QM, reporting, and other management tasks will find it very difficult to grow beyond 150 agents without automating many of these jobs. Contact centers with limited management systems will find it challenging to operate effectively with more than 250 agents, as it will be hard to direct the staff and ensure that they are where they are supposed to be. It is also challenging to manage a virtual contact center with many sites if the contact center director doesn't have visibility into the performance of each site. Every site is different, but efficient management requires both automation and structure.

Contact Center Management Success Checklist

Building a productive and effective contact center that excels at consistently satisfying customers is a combination of art and science. On a relative scale, the "science" component, which involves all contact center systems and infrastructure, is easy. The management aspect of a contact center remains predominantly an "art," even with a growing number of management tools such as QM, WFM, and performance management. Good technologies and applications are necessary enablers and facilitators, but they will never take the place of good management and practices. Here's a checklist to determine if your contact center management is contributing to the success of your contact center.

Yes No

❑   ❑   Do you operate a contact center environment that is open and encourages creativity?

Yes	No	
❏	❏	Is your agent attrition rate below 15 percent annually?
❏	❏	Do you define characteristics of outstanding agents to be used during the hiring process?
❏	❏	Do you test prospective agents before hiring them?
❏	❏	Are 3 to 5 percent of staff-related expenses spent on agent training?
❏	❏	Do agents have an opportunity to evaluate their supervisors and managers (a 360-degree evaluation)?
❏	❏	Do you encourage and reward outstanding quality and customer satisfaction in addition to high productivity?
❏	❏	Does your center employ at least 15 percent part-time staff?
❏	❏	Do you provide frequent (daily or weekly) job performance reports to agents?
❏	❏	Is staff promoted from within whenever possible?

If yours is a world-class contact center that provides outstanding service, your answer will be Yes to every question on this list. If you answered No to more than two of these questions, it's essential to make changes to your operating environment that allow you to immediately convert a No to a Yes. Contact center agents have no reason to tolerate poor management. If you treat your agents well, they will perform for your company and customer satisfaction will be high. If you treat them with indifference, they will leave, but not before they do significant and lasting damage to your customer relationships.

11

Building and Managing Contact Centers

There are numerous ways to acquire contact center infrastructure and agents. The first decision an enterprise must make is whether to build its contact center in-house (or keep it in-house) or to outsource the operation. The second decision, which can impact the first, is whether to purchase, lease, or externally host the systems and applications required to operate the contact center.

Contact center infrastructure can be totally or partially built in-house, outsourced, or hosted, either at the enterprise's site or at a third-party location. Contact centers can be built by the corporation or its consultants, or be acquired completely or in part as a turnkey operation from an outsourcer or ASP. Similarly, contact center staffing resources, including agents, supervisors, managers, and technical support, can be hired directly by an enterprise or indirectly through an outsourcer.

The flexibility of contact center infrastructure has resulted in many hybrid operating environments. These contact centers use a combination of systems purchased and maintained by the enterprise (either in-house or at an outsourcer) along with systems and staffing resources that are being hosted or outsourced.

The four primary approaches (used alone or in combination) for acquiring a contact center are as follows:

1. *Building In-House.* The end user organization takes responsibility for acquiring the real estate, technology, telecommunications, and staffing resources. However, even in this model, consultants may be used to assist with various implementations, such as a CSS application from Siebel, and some or all of the technology can be externally hosted.

2. *Outsourcing.* Some or all of the contact center's infrastructure, technology, or staff is outsourced to a third party. Outsourcing has many models
and may address the entire operation, or just the technology, just the
staff, or a combination of both. In some situations, enterprises elect to
use their own technology infrastructure but the outsourcer's staff, or, in
the opposite case, they may use the outsourcer's infrastructure and their
own staff. In other situations, an outsourcer functions as a backup facility
and receives calls and e-mails only when the enterprise's primary site
exceeds a pre-defined volume threshold. Another scenario will have an
outsourcer performing just one or two functions for an enterprise.
3. *Application Service Provider/Hosting/On Demand.* Some or all applications
are rented from a vendor that generally manages all aspects of the application. As is the case for all of the other options for building contact centers, the exact management of this arrangement varies. In some situations, the application is hosted and managed from the hosting company's
site, and in others, the server may be placed at the primary company's
site but is still managed and operated by the hosting company. The key
difference between hosting and outsourcing is that in the ASP model, the
hosting company owns and manages the application.
4. *Consulting.* An end-user organization hires one or more consultants to
assist in implementing and/or maintaining a specific application, such as
WFM, or improving a process, such as enhancing customer loyalty, or in
building and maintaining the entire operation. Consultants are generally
used to complement existing internal resources.

The Pros and Cons of Different Acquisition Models

There are many options available for obtaining assistance in building contact centers. Each of these approaches includes benefits and disadvantages
for the enterprise, as is reflected in Figure 11.1.

Changes in business model, rapid growth, corporate expense pressure,
mergers and acquisitions, and consolidations force contact center managers to continuously review the options for providing the best service at
the lowest cost. This forces managers to determine if they should keep or
build contact centers in-house, outsource, or host. And, if the choice is to
outsource, a company must decide whether to do so in their primary geog-
raphy or use an offshore outsourcer.

Figure 11.1: Contact Center Acquisition Model Pros and Cons

Acquisition Model	Pro	Con
Building In-House	• Own your investment. • Can customize at will. • On-site resources to respond quickly to your business requirements. • Once depreciated, no additional capital costs. • Cost effective if contact center will be owned and operated for more than three years.	• Need to purchase hardware on which to run. • Ties up capital. • Requires IT and business staff to run and maintain operating environment. • Depending on size of investment, will likely require a lengthy senior management approval process. • Continuous management challenge to maintain and enhance the contact center.
Outsourcing	• Removes assets from company books and reduces capital budget, overhead, and staff counts. • Allows an enterprise to concentrate on core competencies instead of service delivery. • Can greatly reduce start-up time, as many outsourcing facilities are already built and ready to take on new business. • Should reduce functional management burden.	• Presents new management challenges, as the final responsibility resides with end user organization, but direct management performed by third party. • Loss of functional control. • Can't make immediate changes to process. • Costs are often underestimated and can be more expensive than building and maintaining in-house. • Can be difficult and/or costly if function is later brought back in house or moved to a different vendor.
ASP/Hosting/On Demand	• Minimizes need for hardware and IT support. • Rapid deployment. • Does not require large up-front capital investment.	• If hosting for more than 2 1/2 years, will likely cost an enterprise more than if purchased. • Generally harder to customize and enterprise

	• New application releases installed with minimal user involvement. • Easy to deploy in multiple sites. • Generally accesses operational budget instead of capital budget so approval process is quicker. • Shared best practices.	does not own customizations. • Challenging to integrate with other corporate systems. • Potential for greater security concerns. • Dependent upon a third party.
Consulting	• Brings domain expertise and shared best practices. • Facilitates knowledge transfer to internal staff. • Provides resources for rapid deployment. • Can augment staff and provide expertise not resident in the company.	• Can be expensive. • Possibly results in accountability issues. • May lead to lack of in-house knowledge about critical infrastructure. • Often end up teaching consultants your business. • Have to retrain resources when consultants transition to new jobs.

Source: DMG Consulting LLC.

Building an In-House Contact Center

It takes a great deal of time, money, and expertise to build a leading-edge contact center. The cost will vary based on a center's size, purpose, service level, technology requirements, and location. As an example, it will typically cost between $1 million and $10 million to build a 250-seat contact center. (As many contact centers start small and grow, the costs are generally not incurred in year 1 but add up over time.) And it will cost $1 million to $3 million annually to operate a 250-person contact center, including real estate, telecom, agents, system maintenance, and depreciation expenses.

Enterprises typically want to own any function that is considered a core competency. So if the contact center is thought to be fundamental to business operations and service delivery, an enterprise will likely want to own its contact center resources. Building and operating contact centers in-house can be highly beneficial, as it gives the enterprise direct and immediate control over this critical service delivery organization. The downside is that an in-house contact center requires a large up-front investment and a great deal of staff. And once the center is built, continuous enhancements and ongoing investments in people and technology are critical to maintaining a competitive edge. As the majority of its interactions are real-time, the contact center must be highly flexible and adaptable to change. Building a dynamic operating environment requires knowledgeable leaders and the support of senior management.

Factors Critical to the Success of an In-House Center

Whether building a new in-house contact center or upgrading an existing one, following these eleven steps will promote success:

1. *Draft a document reflecting your corporate vision or goals.* Investments should be made only if they fill an important business need. The vision may be to provide outstanding service in all channels, enhance self-service options, convert a cost center to a profit center, take advantage of real-time sales opportunities, evolve to an engaged real-time contact center, or be a low-cost provider.
2. *Determine contact center needs.* After documenting corporate goals, identify the specific systems, processes, and staffing needs for your contact center. There are over 50 systems that can be used in contact centers, but not all are required by every center. Limit the scope of the project to better your chances for success.
3. *Obtain support and buy-in from senior management, stakeholders, and constituents.* Making investments and changes in contact centers will take time and money and impact stakeholders and constituents. Getting buy-in for changes from all relevant parties is critical for the success of the project and for the future of the contact center. (A new system to improve up-selling and cross-selling by the contact center will not realize the greatest benefits if not supported by sales and marketing.)
4. *Identify costs and benefits.* Prioritize projects based on their payback and contribution to the enterprise. Projects with a rapid payback and low TCO will encourage the support and interest of senior management and stakeholders.
5. *Request budget approval.* Most companies have standard guidelines for

requesting budget approval. Work within the system, even if it slows down your project, as it ensures the support of senior management and sets you up to receive credit for your contributions to the company's success.

6. *Draft a business and technical project plan.* Write a detailed project plan that addresses all business and technical requirements. It's essential to address technology, processes, and people in the plan.

7. *Acquire expertise.* Hire new employees or consultants or retrain existing staff to assist with the implementations.

8. *Build or implement.* Either build or enhance the contact center by implementing new systems or modifying existing ones. The development and implementation teams should include both technical and business representatives to address technology, people, and process.

9. *Hire and train new staff.* When building or enlarging a contact center, it's important to hire and train management, supervisors, and agents to handle additional transaction volume or new functions being supported by the contact center. The business staff should work with corporate human resources (HR) to make sure that the staff is hired and trained on a timely basis, so that they are ready to handle increased volume once the center is up and running. (It's also important for hiring and training not to occur too far in advance, as it's very expensive to maintain staff that is not handling transactions.)

10. *Test and implement.* Once the staff is ready, the new contact center, system, or function should be fully tested before being put into production. Once fully tested and properly staffed, the new functionality or process should be implemented and monitored very carefully for the first few weeks. All staff should be invited to provide feedback.

11. *Build an information feedback loop.* The best contact centers are always looking for ways to improve their operations. Build both formal and informal feedback processes to ensure that all employee and customer insights are captured and utilized.

Determining if Outsourcing Is the Right Choice for You

As the cost of building and maintaining leading-edge contact centers grows and outsourcers are building increasingly compelling operating environments, more enterprises are outsourcing contact center activities. The last 3 years have seen a surge in contact center outsourcing, as companies realized that they could save money, particularly in offshore locations (if the implementation was done cleanly).

Factors Affecting Outsourcing Location

More than 200,000 contact center seats have been moved to offshore locations, including Canada, India, Mexico, Puerto Rico, and the Philippines, where agent costs are 25 to 80 percent less than in the United States. The migration of activity offshore has been so great that many leading contact center outsourcers have built facilities in a number of overseas locations.

Use the table in Figure 11.2 to determine if you should outsource in the United States, Canada, or in an offshore location.

Offshore outsourcing is a politically charged but financially beneficial alternative. All issues discussed in this chapter are relevant to offshore outsourcing. However, outsourcing offshore has additional challenges. See Chapter 12 for more on offshore outsourcing.

Deciding What Functions to Outsource

Once you decide that outsourcing is your optimum alternative, it's time to decide which aspects of the contact center to outsource. Options include:

- Entire contact center
- Technology infrastructure
- Staff
- Overflow
- Backup
- Contingency

All outsourcing relationships require management overhead and oversight. Outsourcers are often very dedicated but need attention, just like any individual or department within the company. Keep in mind that the management aspect of the relationship does not end once the outsourcing agreement is signed. It takes a great deal of work to manage and maintain an outsourcing relationship that benefits the enterprise, its customers, and the outsourcer on an ongoing basis.

Figure 11.2: Selecting an Outsourcing Location

Geographical Regions	Outsource to This Location if:	*Do Not* Outsource to This Location if:
United States	• Product is complex. • There are cultural issues. • Service providers must have U.S. accents. • Government regulations or politics force you to keep your function in the United States. • You are new to outsourcing and want the company and the contact center to be geographically close. • Cost savings are not your highest corporate priority.	• You are not compelled by corporate or regulatory requirements to have a contact center in the United States and cost reduction is the highest priority. (United States–based outsourcers are some of the most expensive in the world—with the exception of contact centers operated by the Department of Justice.)
Canada	• Reducing servicing costs is a priority, but you still want to provide service similar to United States. • Service requires North American accents and culture. • Stable politics are a requirement. • Contact center needs to be geographically close to United States–based business.	• Cost is not the main concern, as the savings are not large and depend upon the relative strength of the Canadian dollar.
Offshore	• Cost is highest priority. • You are able and willing to locate management staff offshore to oversee the operation. • You are willing to work closely with outsourcer to set up your operation and ensure that agents are properly trained and fully understand the needs of your customers.	• You are in a highly political operating environment, such as a federal or state contact center. • Public relations are a high priority.

Source: DMG Consulting LLC.

Outsourcing the Entire Contact Center

Outsourcing the entire operation may indicate that you believe the outsourcer has better domain expertise, technology, agents, and management than your organization, but it may just mean that the outsourcer has a lower cost structure. It also generally indicates that the outsourcer has made a cost-effective bid for your business. It's fine to outsource an entire contact center, but the success of the outsourcing arrangement depends upon your company continuing to take ownership of the function, even when the day-to-day operations are handled by a third party. If customers are dissatisfied with service quality they are going to blame your company, not the outsourcers, and possibly even cancel their account. The best outsourcers will therefore be open to the primary company's active participation and oversight.

Outsourcing Technology Infrastructure

Companies that believe that people are the main differentiator between service organizations will want to continue to "own" their staff, but will not necessarily want to invest in or maintain the technology. There are three primary ways that these priorities can be accommodated:

1. A company can hire and train contact center staff at its own campus and then place them at the outsourcer's site.
2. A company can hire and train contact center staff at the outsourcer's site. Some companies combine approaches, and others even make a deal contingent upon an outsourcer taking their staff along with the technology infrastructure.
3. An enterprise can sell its technology infrastructure to an outsourcer and require the outsourcer to "buy" its existing staff.

Outsourcing Staff

Some companies are very comfortable with their technology infrastructure but decide that the contact center is no longer a core competency for them. In these situations, the enterprise will require the outsourcer either to replicate their systems environment or to take and install their systems. The enterprise will leave the management of agents to the outsourcer, but may also provide agent training programs.

Outsourcing Overflow

Often companies sign up an outsourcer to handle call or e-mail volume that exceeds their projections. This is a great way to ensure that service levels are met, but it requires a large investment for what may be little benefit. Keep in mind that the outsourcer's staff has to be fully trained and prepared, even if they receive only one call per day.

Outsourcing Backup and Contingency

Many companies have arranged backup and contingency arrangements with contact centers that specialize in this area. This gives the company access to an operating contact center when theirs is shut down. This is a great approach, but companies must monitor this relationship on an ongoing basis to ensure that the backup site is up to date on all system upgrades and processes.

Determining Term of Outsourcing Agreement

Outsourcers want to establish long-term contracts, which are not always in the best interest of the end user. For end users, it's better to set up an agreement with a shorter duration for added flexibility, which is one of the reasons for setting up an outsourcing arrangement to begin with. But keep in mind that outsourcers invest a great deal on start-up efforts, including system installation and integration, staffing, and training, much of which is not immediately or directly recovered. So outsourcers want to be sure that an agreement lasts long enough for them to recover their start-up costs.

Contact center outsourcers are looking to set up contracts for a minimum of 2 years and often as much as 5 years, while end users would be better off with 1-year agreements with the right to renew. But trade-offs can be negotiated. Outsourcers will generally compromise on the term of the agreement if an end user is willing to pay larger transaction fees, a greater share of the start-up costs, or a cancellation penalty. The trade-off is then between flexibility and cost.

Outsourcing Best Practices

Surprisingly, the easy part of outsourcing is selecting a vendor that can meet your company's service, quality, and customer satisfaction requirements, is an appropriate cultural match (whether you remain on shore or go offshore), and is priced right. The selection process is a dating ritual where both parties are on their best behavior. Once the deal is completed and the agreement signed, each company's true personality comes out and the real work begins. Making the relationship work takes a lot of effort, good planning, and compromise, as no vendor can satisfy 100 percent of your corporate requirements on an ongoing basis. Here is a list of best practices to ensure ongoing success throughout your outsourcing relationship:

1. Do not base your selection solely on price.
2. Select an outsourcer whose culture and service philosophy match those of your organization, even if the outsourcer is not the lowest-cost provider.
3. Select an outsourcer that can satisfy your company's data requirements and security concerns.
4. Do not begin working with the outsourcer until the agreement is signed.
5. If technological innovation is important to your company, select an outsourcer that has a track record of implementing innovative systems on an ongoing basis.
6. Include in your agreement the right to enhance the systems environment on a periodic basis.
7. If systems infrastructure is critical for your company, maintain its ownership and outsource management of the contact center.
8. Define and include a detailed service level agreement (SLA) in your outsourcing agreement. However, establish a process for modifying the SLA on a periodic basis so that it remains current and can address changing priorities of your corporation and its customers. The SLA must be a living document that changes with the times. A lot will change during the 3- to 5-year life of a typical outsource contract. (See the SLA section of Chapter 12.)
9. Define roles and responsibilities of primary team members to ensure that all relationship expectations are met. For example, if you expect to have a dedicated account or relationship manager, ask for one in your agreement.
10. Establish escalation procedures for the outsourcer stating when a customer issue should be brought to the attention of your company. Outsourcers are representatives of your company and should be able to address the vast majority—more than 99 percent—of all customer issues, but they must have the option of escalating an inquiry to your company when needed. Be sure that a customer can reach your company when necessary or you will end up losing business. The ultimate responsibility for the treatment of every customer remains with your company.

11. Establish formal and informal processes for ensuring continuous knowledge transfer between your company and the outsourcer. Many companies develop formal processes for the start-up and then neglect ongoing knowledge sharing and transfer. A great deal is going to change over the duration of your relationship, and it's essential to ensure that information is shared on a timely basis.
12. Define quality and customer satisfaction and exactly how you expect your customers to be treated. Provide detailed training programs or assist the outsourcer in doing so.
13. Survey customers on a periodic basis to make sure that customer satisfaction is not decreasing as a result of the outsourcer's service quality. Do not ask the outsourcer's agents to conduct the survey, as that could be a conflict of interest.
14. Meet with the outsourcer's agents on a periodic basis and learn directly from them what is happening with your customers. This will give you direct feedback about your customers' satisfaction. Showing the outsourcer's agents that you care about them will also improve service.
15. Reward your outsourcer and its agents for providing excellent service. Don't take it for granted, even if it is required by your agreement.
16. Receive daily feedback from your outsourcer on essential issues; do not ask your outsourcer to hold feedback for once-a-week meetings.
17. Set up a real-time feedback loop from the outsourcer to your organization to ensure that your company receives timely insights from its customers. This can be done with real-time analytics, speech analytics, and performance management. (See Chapter 9 for more on real-time analytics.)
18. Use a contact center performance management system to ensure that all corporate objectives are being met on a daily basis. (See Chapter 7 for more on performance management.)

Even when best practices are applied, outsourcers are capable of providing good service to your customers, but are generally not considered world-class service organizations. Most are not positioned to change their systems and practices frequently enough to maintain a differentiating service advantage, which is required of world-class operating environments. Companies dedicated to providing world-class service must either develop a unique relationship with an outsourcer or keep their contact center in-house.

Best Practices for the Outsourcing Transition

Outsourcers generally have detailed checklists and project plans to assist enterprises in transitioning their business. During the selection process, make sure that your company is comfortable with the outsourcer's transition plan. If you are not, negotiate a more favorable one. And if the outsourcer is so new that a transition plan does not exist or the outsourcer is not flexible about making the changes required by your company, assess if this is a vendor you want to work with on an ongoing basis.

Here are eleven key steps you can take to effectively manage the outsourcing transition:

1. Define ownership of the transition process and plan. Primary responsibility should be in the hands of two people, one from your company and one from the outsourcer.
2. Establish a transition plan of record for the project. Put in place a process for approving and managing changes to the plan.
3. Work together to develop a plan that satisfies your company and the outsourcer before beginning the transition. Don't rush the planning. Thinking through all of the steps and making sure everything is set before beginning the transition will save time, money, effort, and customer disruption and dissatisfaction.
4. Communicate openly, accurately, and frequently about the outsourcing transition with your internal staff. Also provide agents with information on other options that may be open to them within the company as well as any services you will make available to them to ease the transition. When agents lose jobs to an outsourcer, whether in the United States or abroad, there are a lot of hard feelings, but a considerate and open approach on your part can minimize this. Further, when agents are not informed, they will make up their own answers when customers ask about changes in service.
5. If possible, provide a bonus during the transition period to internal agents who stay and perform their jobs well. This will motivate agents to remain with your company until the end.
6. If practical, find internal jobs for contact center staff displaced due to the outsourcing. Many contact center agents can add great value to your company because of their in-depth knowledge of your business.

7. Offer to transfer willing and outstanding agents to the outsourcer. (This will provide domain expertise to the outsourcer.)

8. Provide a financial package and/or job placement services to employees displaced by the outsourcing to minimize the negative impact.

9. Draft a communication that outsourcing agents can share with customers who ask about the change. In some situations, a new accent makes it obvious that a change has taken place. Agents should not volunteer this information, but they also shouldn't hide it if asked by customers.

10. Shift the transaction volume to the outsourcer in logical increments, instead of all at once, if the volume is high or includes multiple channels. For example, if service includes e-mail and phone support, first shift the e-mail function and make sure the outsourcer does an adequate job before moving the phone calls.

11. Do not close down the old contact center until you are sure that the new outsourcer is functioning properly and has proven that it can handle inquiries. It might cost a few dollars to have two contact centers running at the same time, but it can save a great deal of money and prevent lost customers. (The old center should remain functional with a skeleton crew for 1 to 2 weeks after the transfer.)

Maintaining the Real-Time Advantage Using an Outsourcer

Outsourcers present many advantages but also new challenges for companies. It's difficult to build and maintain a real-time environment when working with an outsourcer, as there is a third party involved. As real-time information is a strong competitive advantage for companies, maintaining this advantage, even in an outsourcing business model, could be critical to the success of a company.

Setting up a real-time information flow when working with an outsourcer involves innovation in both process and systems and is likely to cost your organization extra fees, as it is not a standard offering. While an outsourcer can provide real-time reporting relatively easily, if you are looking for customer insights based on analysis and understanding of unstructured phone conversations and e-mails in real or near-real time, you will have to set up both manual and automated processes so that the outsourcer can capture and share this information. (See Chapter 9 on real-time analytics.)

Contact Center Outsourcing Market

The contact center outsourcing market is large and growing and consists of hundreds of vendors.

- *Large IT Outsourcers.* These vendors do all types of IT outsourcing, including contact centers, and have operations in and out of the United States. These vendors are Affiliated Computer Services (ACS), Inc., Computer Sciences Corporation (CSC), Electronic Data Systems Corporation (EDS), Hewlett-Packard (HP) Services, IBM Global Services, Perot Systems, and Unisys.
- *Contact Center Outsourcers.* These vendors specialize in providing contact center outsourcing. United States–based vendors include APAC Teleservices, cccInteractive, Convergys, ICT Group, Interact, Inc., Interactive Response Technologies, Inc., NCO Group, OKS-Ameridial, Precision Response Corporation, Protocol Communications, RMH Teleservices, Sitel Corporation, Source One Communications Inc., Stream International, Sykes, Teleperformance, Telespectrum, Teletch, The Faneuil Group, Telvista, and West Corporation. These companies vary in size, number of sites, and geographical locations. Some have one contact center and others have dozens located around the world. Canada-based vendors include Alliance Call Centre Services, Client Logic Inc., Minacs Worldwide Inc., Nordia, NuComm International Inc., Omega Direct Response Inc., and Vox Data.
- *Offshore Outsourcers.* These contact center vendors are located in other regions of the world. A list of vendors can be found in Chapter 12.

Hosted Solution: On-Demand Application Service Providers

Application service providers host hardware or software for end-user organizations. A hosted solution is one that is rented or leased from a vendor for a specific time period. It is also referred to as on-demand hardware and/or software or an on-demand solution provider. During the term of a hosting agreement, which is frequently 1 to 2 years (but can be any duration), the end user can use the hosted product and can choose to integrate it with its own internal systems. Once the contract ends, ownership of the application and any custom development done on it for the end user revert to the hosting company.

A few years ago, hosted offerings were functionally inferior to licensed offerings, as many vendors saw hosting as a quick way to come to market with a functionally or technically weak product. However, since 2002, vendors in many markets have started to use hosting as an alternative sales channel to penetrate companies that wanted to avoid making a capital investment or didn't have in-house resources to maintain the application. As a result, many strong products are now being sold as hosted offerings. This also forced stand-alone hosting vendors to offer functionally and technically strong products in order to be competitive.

Integrating Hosting into a Contact Center Environment

One of the major advantages of the ASP/on-demand business model is the simplicity with which it can be integrated into a contact center environment, since many hosting companies are experienced in basic integrations to primary contact center technologies. Further, there is little upfront investment—generally just a relatively small start-up fee. And the monthly hosting fee is an operational expense that can often be covered with little incremental impact on a department's budget.

The challenging part of on-demand computing occurs when the hosted application needs to be integrated into a department's operational system to realize its full benefits. Most hosting companies have technical resources to do the integration, if you are willing to pay for it. The issue is that integration expenses are a throwaway because your company does not own the product.

Security is a second major concern corporations have about hosting, as a third party owns the application that the customer data reside on. This is a real issue and one that hosting companies are addressing and continuously working to improve. All hosting companies offer a number of increasingly sophisticated security options for their customers.

Is Hosting Suitable for Your Contact Center?

Hosting is a viable alternative to premise-based or outsourced contact center infrastructure. Select a hosted offering if any of the following applies:

- You need a system or application but do not have a budget to purchase it.
- You need a system or application but do not have IT resources to install and maintain the system.
- You have a geographically dispersed user base and do not have or want to create the necessary support infrastructure.
- A lease-versus-buy analysis indicates that it is a good financial decision.
- You need to implement a new system quickly and don't have time to do an on-site installation.
- You want to stay current with technological innovations but do not want to do system upgrades.
- You have a short-term need for a system or application.
- You want to try out an application to be sure that it works and adds the expected value before making a large investment.
- The hosted solution has all of the functionality that you need and cannot be licensed.
- You want your outsourcer to use a specific system or application but the outsourcer is not yet ready to make the investment.
- You are a small or mid-size contact center and are not satisfied with licensed offerings.

Contact Center Hosting Market: What's Available

Almost all contact center infrastructure, technology, systems, and applications are available in a hosted business model. This includes everything from core ACD infrastructure that can be leased through NSPs such as British Telecom (BT), Deutsche Telecom, France Telecom, Japan Telecom, NTT Telecom, or large contact center outsourcers such as Convergys or West Corporation, to quality management and recording that is now available on an ASP basis from VoiceLog LLC. We estimate that by the end of 2005 more than 55 percent of all contact centers will use one or more hosted systems.

Application service providers are making a concerted effort to deliver products for the small and mid-size marketplace, which larger contact center vendors neglected for years. As a result, these vendors hold a strong market presence in this sector. In 2003, the larger "enterprise" vendors also started to deliver more appropriately priced and targeted offerings for small and mid-size companies.

When to Use Consultants

Consultants can add a great deal of value, filling skill or resource gaps in an organization. Consulting options are varied, ranging from large consulting firms with dedicated contact center practices to medium-size boutique firms specializing in contact centers to independent consultants. Use consulting services if any of the following applies:

- Your company needs a specific expertise and/or experience level that it does not have and cannot or does not want to hire full-time employees to do.
- Your company needs incremental resources for a specific job. As consultants can be viewed as temporary employees, they are frequently hired when an organization needs to scale up temporarily for a project.
- Your company wants a second, unbiased opinion about a project.
- Your company needs a job done that will likely be viewed negatively by employees, such as leading a downsizing or offshore outsourcing initiative. Consultants can be used so management can distance itself from the project, allowing a quick return to business as usual.

Tricks for Successfully Managing Consultants

Consultants can bring great expertise and skill to a job and often work complementarily with an enterprise. However, consultants make a living from having lots of engagements and, as a result, they are always looking for their next project. This means that while they are doing the job for you they may be on the lookout for other opportunities to sell their services to you. Although this isn't necessarily negative, it is something that has to be managed through internal oversight.

Consultants generally bring a process and methodology for accomplishing your goals—their experience might be a significant reason for hiring them. If you want the consulting expertise but not the consultants' standard methodology, be sure to communicate this before you hire them. In the larger consulting firms, process is tied to how staff is trained and promoted and how clients are billed. If you expect anything different, be sure to include it in your consulting agreement.

To be highly successful and keep the costs down, you must carefully manage all consulting engagements, or your company will likely experience cost overruns. Consultants are not "out to get" the company they are doing work for, but their methodology often includes steps that are not necessary for your project, or their priorities may differ from those of your company. Avoid this issue and project "creep"—where a project cannot be completed on time either because of changing customer requirements or because a consultant underestimated in an effort to win a bid—by carefully defining all specifications and assigning internal staff to manage the consultants.

Best Practices for Managing Consulting Engagements

Consultants can make significant contributions to a contact center, but their activities must be properly managed to ensure that they stay on track with defined project goals. Follow these best practices to optimize the results of your consulting arrangement:

1. Assign a strong and respected internal manager or team to oversee all consulting and system integration projects.
2. Do not let the consultants take ownership of a project. They can lead it, but final approval must always come from your management. (This will help to avoid project "creep.")
3. Hire specific individuals within a firm to do a job, not just a firm or partner. Most consulting firms have a limited number of experienced domain experts. These people are in high demand, and the consulting firms will use them to start a project and realize early wins. The consulting firms will want to move these experts to the next engagement as quickly as possible. Make sure the people you hire are named in your agreement and are required to stay on your project until the hand-off is complete.
4. When considering a large consulting firm, check out its reputation—operationally, interpersonally, and technically—before inviting the firm to participate in an RFP.
5. Check the references of the individuals you are planning to hire to make sure that they have the required expertise, are pleasant to work with, and will fit into your organization's culture.
6. Request a list of technology vendor partnerships from all consulting firms you are considering. The consulting firms are financially motivated to use their partners' products in deals. So, for example, if a consulting firm has a partnership with Avaya for contact center infrastruc-

ture and Siebel for CRM application functionality, they will probably recommend these two vendors. If your company does not want to use the consulting firm's partners, let them know that you'd prefer other options at the outset of the project.

7. Specify and document the job requirements to avoid misunderstanding.

8. Define exactly what job completion means in the contract to avoid disagreements and dissatisfaction.

9. Separate projects into measurable phases and re-evaluate the consultant's or consulting firm's job performance after each phase. Each phase must include milestones.

10. Include a "right to cancel" clause in your consulting agreement. There are many reasons, from change in business needs or strategy, to financial issues, to dissatisfaction, that may cause your company to want to cancel the agreement. To avoid conflict and hassle, address these issues in your agreement before beginning the work. Of course, your company must be fair about paying the consultants for work completed.

11. Use consultants to build internal expertise so your company can maintain the project once it is complete and handed off. If possible, include internal staff on the consulting teams and require knowledge transfer during the project to ensure that the consultants can leave when the project is done. Many consultants will tell you that including internal staff on their teams will slow them down, or they will relegate internal staff to non-essential tasks that do not provide knowledge transfer. Good consultants will be happy to work with your staff to ensure knowledge transfer, as they prefer their work to succeed on an ongoing basis. (This is more of an issue with system integration firms than with strategy firms.)

12. Specify the transition process and time frames in the agreement. Consulting firms may take shortcuts or skip the transition process to meet deadlines or to move staff along to the next job. If the hand-off is done too quickly and your staff is not trained adequately, your company may end up having to call back the consulting firm to provide ongoing support.

Controlling Consulting Costs

Consultants often charge a premium for their services and time. If an individual consultant or a consulting firm meets or exceeds customer expectations, then they are worth the cost. It can get tricky and often unpleasant when there is project "creep." The goal is to avoid the blame game completely by addressing all of these issues in the agreement before the start of the project. There are two primary pricing techniques used:

1. *Fixed Price.* A consultant bids a set price for a project. This transfers the project risk to the consultant, who will have to absorb the costs of any additional time and complete project-related tasks required by the client. Therefore, a fixed-price engagement must include a detailed specification or statement of all work to be performed. Additionally, there must be a defined process for negotiating any additional work requested by the customer that was not part of the original plan.
2. *Time and Materials (T&M).* A consulting firm charges on an hourly, daily, or weekly basis, plus out-of-pocket expenses. Consulting firms prefer this method as it places the risk on the hiring enterprise and ensures that they are paid for all of their time. Time and materials agreements can turn into nightmares for companies that do not properly size a project or have project requirements that continuously change. Unanticipated costs can double or triple the cost of the effort.

There are risks in both types of pricing techniques, but by carefully defining project and/or system requirements, you can avoid misunderstandings and complete projects successfully. This is the primary goal for both consulting firms and their customers. Negotiating contracts and writing specifications are not always priorities because they appear to delay projects. However, the reality is exactly the opposite. Fully documenting project requirements, deliverables, time frames, and the working relationship between the two companies in an agreement prevents misunderstanding and greatly enhances the chances of project success.

Consulting Market

The contact center consulting market is large and growing. There are three primary categories of contact center consultants: strategy consultants, business consultants, and system integrators. Many firms provide all three types of services.

1. *Large Players.* These vendors have large consulting practices that include a contact center practice. Vendors include Accenture Ltd., BearingPoint, Inc., Cap Gemini, Electronic Data Systems Corporation (EDS),

Deloitte, Ernst and Young (E&Y), IBM Global Services, and McKinsey and Company, Inc.

2. *Contact Center Specialists.* An increasing number of contact center technology providers offer contact center consulting services for their products and services. These vendors include Alcatel, Aspect Communications Corporation, Avaya Inc., Bell Canada, British Telecom (BT), Genesys Telecommunications Laboratories, Inc, IBM Global Services, NICE Systems, Nortel Networks, Nuance, Scansoft/Speechworks Inc., Siemens AG, and Witness Systems.

3. *Small/Mid-Size Consulting Firms.* Answerthink, Inc., Cambridge Technology Partners (owned by Novell, Inc.), DMG Consulting LLC, eLoyalty Corporation, Gold Systems Inc., Incoming Calls Management Institute (ICMI), Telus, Vanguard Communications Corporation, and ZAMBA Corporation.

There are many contact center specialty consulting firms that concentrate on one segment of the market, such as hiring, e-learning, WFM, IVR/speech recognition, contact center design, QM, outsourcing, or outdialing.

Building In-House Versus Outsourcing Checklist

There are many factors to consider when choosing a contact center solution for your organization, such as budget and staffing resources. Use this checklist to assist your company in deciding whether building a contact center in-house or outsourcing services is the right approach.

Yes No

❏ ❏ Does your company have the budget to make the large up-front investment required to build a contact center?

❏ ❏ Is your management willing to place incremental capital investments and people assets on the corporate books?

❏ ❏ Do you have the internal expertise to build and maintain a contact center?

❏ ❏ Do you have adequate time to build a contact center?

❏ ❏ Are you planning on keeping the contact center for at least 5 years?

(continues)

Yes	No	
❏	❏	Is the contact center considered a core competency for your company?
❏	❏	Is the contact center integral to your company's sales strategy?
❏	❏	Can you find skilled resources to staff an in-house contact center?
❏	❏	Does the region where your contact center will be located have a large base of employable people?
❏	❏	Does your company's senior management have customer satisfaction goals?

If you answered No to two or more questions, then your organization should consider outsourcing some or all of your contact center operations. However, as organizational needs change frequently, you should reevaluate your outsourcing decision annually.

12

Navigating the Offshore Landscape

Offshore outsourcing is a hot topic for contact centers because—if done right—it can reduce operating expenses by 50 to 60 percent. It's an option that most enterprises should explore when the service and support function does not need to be co-located with other company activities. But, while the economic benefits are great for companies that execute well, the risks are also significant.

Countries like India, with more than 270 offshore sites (as of February 2004), are confronting many of the same challenges that U.S. contact centers have been facing for years, including high agent attrition rates (up to 60 percent), the need to attract and retain valuable employees, increasing salaries, and the unending cycle of hiring and training. However, even with the increasing salaries that contact centers in India, for example, are paying to retain agents, their rates are still 50 to 80 percent below those paid in the United States. Although the economic benefits are compelling, they must be weighed against the challenges in outsourcing contact center activities in general, which are exacerbated when there are geographical and cultural differences.

The Offshore Outsourcing Economics Argument

It is hard to argue against the numbers. On average, contact center staffing costs USD$30 to $60 per hour per agent in the United States but only USD$13 to $18 per hour per agent in India and the Philippines. (See Figure 12.1.) Contact centers in India and the Philippines are certainly cost competitive, although rates in India, for example, should increase during the next few years due to competition for good agents.

The cost per agent varies based on the complexity and volume of transactions (calls and e-mails). Calls for collections are the least complex and

Figure 12.1: Outsourcing Country Cost Comparison

Country	Cost/hour/person (USD)
Argentina	13 to 16
Australia	25 to 32
Barbados	14 to 16
Canada	17 to 30
Caribbean	18 to 22
China	13 to 15
Columbia	15 to 18
Eastern Europe	8 to 25
India	13 to 18
Mexico	13 to 15
The Philippines	13 to 18
Puerto Rico	18 to 22
United States	30 to 60

Source: Compiled from various industry sources (July 2004).

expensive, while technical support costs are the most challenging and costly. Most offshore contact centers in India, the Philippines, and other countries are multichannel, handling both calls and e-mails. In general, though, the cost of handling e-mails is less than the cost of handling phone calls.

Not-So-Hidden Outsourcing Costs

Many offshore outsourcers bundle telecom, training, and other expenses into their cost per hour per agent, to keep the cost structure simple. However, this may change as offshore outsourcing becomes more popular, allowing for more aggressive and sophisticated pricing schemes. Companies considering outsourcing must ask about all cost components before making a site decision.

It is also important to consider the cost and time of travel from the United States or other country to an offshore location. These expenses add up quickly and are required to manage the relationship, despite claims from many outsourcers that on-site visits are not necessary. Travel expenditures vary based on the location of the outsourcer. Figure 12.2 presents the cost categories to include in your ROI decision and budget. This figure gives the costs for a hypothetical company based in Seattle, Washington, that considers outsourcing to Canada, India, or the Philippines. Your company should have a representative visit the outsourcer at least

Figure 12.2: Estimated Travel Expenses (in U.S. dollars)

Site	Canada	India	The Philippines
Air	$400	$1514	$1313
Hotel	$375	$875	$400
Car Rental	$225	$0	$0
Taxis	$125	$500	$500
Food	$350	$500	$400
Monthly Total	$1,475	$3,389	$2,613
Annual Cost	$17,700	$40,668	$31,356
No. of Days/Trip	4	6	5
Air Travel/Flight	4.5 hours	25 to 30 hours	17 to 20 hours

Notes: Assumes 12 trips per year. Airfare prices based on coach fares.
Source: DMG Consulting LLC.

once monthly, particularly early in the relationship, if no manager is based permanently at the offshore site.

Offshoring Trends

Although there has been a lot of movement of contact centers to offshore locations in recent years, there are still companies that want to build contact centers in the United States. Site selection trends are cyclical. Through 2005, expect to see an increasing number of companies "offshoring." But by 2006, a number of companies that moved their contact centers abroad will move them back to their country of origin or "nearshore" to a nearby country.

Nonfinancial Site Selection Criteria

When making a site selection, enterprises must consider non-financial and socioeconomic factors in addition to the costs. It is essential to find an outsourcer that is willing and able to match the culture of your corporation and the needs of your customers. If the culture of the outsourcer is not suitable, the result will be lost customers and bad press, as happened with Dell at the end of 2003, when some of their contact center functions were returned to the United States after too many negative customer service experiences. Enterprises must review the following factors:

- *Accessibility.* How long does it take to travel to the outsourcer?
- *Language.* Does the population in the selected site speak English or the primary language(s) of your customers?

- *Accent.* Is the accent of the support providers acceptable and understandable to your customers?
- *Work Ethic.* Will the staff be willing to do the work required?
- *Customer Focus.* Will the staff be tolerant of negative customer behavior? For example, will agents tolerate rude and belligerent callers?
- *Quality.* Will the quality of service match or exceed service quality previously provided to your customers?
- *Economy.* Is the economy stable or is it in flux?
- *Resources.* Does the country have adequate English (or other language)-speaking and knowledgeable resources to staff a growing number of contact centers?
- *Education.* Is the population of available resources adequately educated to work in a contact center?
- *Infrastructure.* Does the country have stable utilities and highways?
- *Geographic Issues.* Does the country often have monsoons, tornadoes, hurricanes, or other "acts of God" that disrupt service?
- *Government and Politics.* Is the country politically stable?
- *Risk.* Is the country at risk of war or frequent acts of terrorism?
- *Miscellaneous.* Does the contact center staff understand the culture of your company and customers?

(See Figure 12.3 for a comparison of three offshore contact center locations in terms of these factors.)

U.S. companies began outsourcing contact center activities to Canada in the 1990s because the culture was very similar to that of the United States and weakness in the Canadian dollar resulted in savings of 20 to 30 percent. When these financial benefits lessened in the early 2000s (as the Canadian dollar strengthened), corporations found a lower-cost alternative in India, the Philippines, and other locations. While India was then relatively new to contact center outsourcing, the country had already been doing systems development outsource work for years.

Offshore Contact Center Models

There are many types of offshore contact center models. Enterprises need to decide which type to use before beginning the selection process. The four primary offshore contact center models are:

Figure 12.3: Country Socioeconomic Comparison

	Canada	India	Philippines
Accessibility	2- to 4-hour time difference.	10-hour time difference.	8-hour time difference.
Language	English is one of 2 national languages—first language for most of population.	English is one of 16 national languages—dominant for commercial and political speech.	English—one of 2 national languages—is spoken by nearly all professional, government, and academic workers.
Accent	Minimal—not noticeable except among French speakers and immigrants.	Very strong and sometimes hard to understand.	Slight and easy to understand.
Work Ethic	Strong.	Strong.	Moderate.
Customer Focus	Similar to United States.	Moderate to weak (for example, not welcoming to rude callers).	Very strong.
Quality	Similar to United States.	Driven to provide correct information.	Relaxed.
Economy	Similar to United States.	Since reforms in 1991, economy has been growing relatively fast and has a large technology sector.	Lapsed Asian tiger—relatively high unemployment (approximately 10%).
Resources	Economy is very similar to that of the United States, except more dependent on natural resources.	1 billion people, middle class of 150 million, college-educated people interested in working in contact centers.	Population of 85 million, 10 million in Metro Manila.
Education	Similar to United States.	Has large numbers of well-educated people skilled in English. Big exporter of computer software.	Good basic education with 95% literacy rate.
Infrastructure	Similar to United States.	Poor. Electricity not dependable. Make sure site has diesel back-up generator.	Frequent power and utility outages. Make sure site has diesel backup generator.
Geographic Issues	Similar to United States.	Frequent heavy rains and monsoons. Very hot.	Volcanic island group.
Government and Politics	Similar to United States.	Longstanding, diverse democracy. Problems with ethnic conflicts and border wars.	Unstable government. Recurring problems with Muslim insurgencies and corruption.
Risk	Similar to United States.	Moderate. Ongoing clashes and skirmishes near borders. Occasional local outbreaks of ethnic unrest.	Very high. Foreigners at risk of kidnapping. High crime rate in cities.
Miscellaneous	Understand how Americans do business.	Caste system profoundly affects the country's behavioral norms. Major regional differences in infrastructure and business friendliness.	Understand how Americans do business.

Source: DMG Consulting LLC.

1. *United States–Based and Owned.* Many United States–based outsourcers have built centers in India, the Philippines, and other countries. The cost of these centers is generally higher than for domestically owned centers, but they offer more United States–based culture.

2. *United States–Owned.* United States-based companies own centers in many countries. In some cases, an outsourcer established the center in its

own country and decided to incorporate in the United States. In other cases, U.S. business people decided to set up an offshore outsourcing business.

3. *Domestically Owned.* A large and growing number of contact centers around the world are domestically owned.

4. *Captive.* A captive center is one that is dedicated to a particular company. There are a few captive models. The first is where a foreign company builds and operates its own contact center. The second is where a foreign company builds its own contact center but hires local talent to operate it. And a third is where a domestic outsourcer builds a contact center, but the entire center is dedicated to one business.

Contact Center Selection Process

Offshore outsourcing companies and sites are proliferating throughout the world, and corporations that decide to locate their contact center activities offshore have many good choices. Companies need to narrow down the regions and countries where they are willing to operate before selecting an outsourcer. To achieve this goal, corporations must begin the selection process by developing an analytic framework that addresses both economic and socioeconomic factors. They must also seriously consider risk factors and eliminate countries where the perils are too great. For example, if the threat of war, terrorism, kidnapping, or social unrest is too risky for your company, then eliminate from your list all the countries where these problems are endemic. You can find country risk factors at two web sites—the Central Intelligence Agency's World Fact Book, http://www.cia.gov/cia/publications/factbook/index.html, and the U.S. State Department's Background Notes, http://www.state.gov/r/pa/ei/bgn/. It is also always a good idea to touch base with local contacts in the selected regions to validate the information used in the analysis.

Once you select the candidate offshore locations, research the average cost per hour per agent and all other related expenses. Include all of this data in a site cost analysis that compares the economics of your company's current contact center operation to those of the selected location(s). (See Figure 12.4 for a hypothetical comparison of sites in Canada, India, and the Philippines.)

Once your company selects the location(s) and site model, it is time to

Figure 12.4: Projected Site Cost Analysis

	Current Site	Canada	India	The Philippines
Labor Costs[a]				
Customer Service—Phone	$ 3,680,473	$3,200,411	$1,659,472	$1,659,472
Technical Support—Phone	$ 1,209,425	$1,078,560	$ 539,280	$ 539,280
Customer Service—E-Mail	$ 471,240	$ 445,536	$ 222,768	$ 222,768
Technical Support—E-Mail	$ 609,840	$ 643,104	$ 310,464	$ 310,464
Administration & Coordination Costs[b]				
One FTE	NA	$ 100,000	$ 100,000	$ 100,000
Site Visits (1 per month)	NA	$ 17,700	$ 40,668	$ 31,356
Video Conferencing	NA	$ 40,000	$ 50,000	$ 50,000
Telecom Costs[c]				
Toll-Free Lines	$ 456,000	$ 228,000	$ 228,000	$ 228,000
Long-Distance Circuits	$ 50,400	$ 37,800	$ 37,800	$ 37,800
Total[d]	$ 6,477,378	$5,791,111	$3,188,452	$3,179,140

a. Assumes that productivity and, therefore, required hours will remain the same regardless of location.

b. Assumes that dealing with a geographically remote vendor will require a dedicated support person.

c. Assumes that carrier and circuit costs will be reduced by 50% and by two local and two long-distance circuits; circuits cost $900/month and $200/month, respectively.

d. Assumes no contract termination or conversion charges.

Source: DMG Consulting LLC.

find two or three vendors that meet your business needs. Some countries, like India, have organized a government, quasi-government, or business agency to represent their offshore outsourcing activities. Begin the vendor selection process by looking for representative agencies, speaking to industry analysts, consultants, or colleagues who have already outsourced, and/or by performing searches on the Internet. If it is important for the outsourcer to use a specific vendor's contact center switch (such as Avaya, Nortel, or Siemens) to be in compliance, then get in touch with those vendors and ask them for recommendations in the selected countries.

Creating a Detailed Request for Proposal

While you are gathering the names of viable vendors, begin the process of creating a detailed RFP. An RFP serves many purposes, including:

1. Defining your company's current and future outsourcing requirements.
2. Achieving internal agreement. (While not the primary purpose of an RFP, it is an effective method for gaining enterprise buy-in for an initiative.)
3. Defining the terms and conditions for doing business with an offshore outsourcing partner.
4. Shortening the contract negotiation phase.

The RFP must address the following categories:

- *Financial Viability.* Is the vendor financially stable? Is the outsourcer well-funded, and do they have enough revenue or cash in the bank to be in business for at least another three years?
- *Technology.* Does the vendor have the right technology to support your organization, and does it have well-trained resources who know how to optimize performance? Another consideration is IP. If IP is part of your company's telecom plan, then the vendor must have either IP or an IP-enabled switch.
- *Operations.* Many offshore contact center vendors are very new. Make sure that they know how to build and operate a contact center. And, unless you are willing to spend the time and money to teach them your business, make sure that they have previous experience in your vertical market.
- *Management.* Make sure the contact center has experienced management staff.
- *Staff.* Look carefully at the contact center agents. Assess their education, fluency in the language of your customers, knowledge of the culture where calls and e-mails are coming from, technical skills, level of patience, ability to work with your customer demographics, and willingness to deal with challenging callers. Make sure the staff is competent to deal with the transactions that would be sent to their center (e.g., technical calls, e-mails, account retention, collections, fraud, sales, human resources, internal help desk, etc.).
- *Training.* Take a very close look at the outsourcer's training procedures and the quality of its trainers, as you will have to spend a great deal of time with them. Examine their education, basic training program, how they address culture and accents, up-training and retraining, and how they combine the results of their QM and training programs.

- *Quality Management.* Check if the outsourcer has a formal QM program and, if so, observe it in action. (Many outsourcers say they have a QM program, but it is not always formal or institutionalized.) Ask how frequently agents are coached and retrained. Find out if agents are rewarded for good behavior in addition to being coached to improve techniques. It is strongly recommended that you select an outsourcer that does both call and screen QM. And make sure that you can listen to calls remotely.

- *Escalation Procedures.* Review the center's standard escalation procedures to see if the contact center "gets it." The center must be willing to take ownership of problems but must also be open to reaching out to your company when necessary. Customers must always feel that they can reach your company directly, or you could end up with a press relations problem. Knowing when to escalate and when to resolve a problem internally is a subtlety that comes with experience. Make sure the outsourcer displays this knowledge.

- *Service Level Agreements.* All outsourcers have standard SLAs, and you are almost certainly going to want to change them. Ask the vendor to provide a comprehensive list of SLAs and metrics they report. Give the vendor a complete list of the information and KPIs that your company requires. (See the detailed SLA section that follows.) If a vendor does not already provide the KPIs your company requires, find out what it would cost for them to do so.

- *Reporting.* Review the vendor's standard reports. Give vendors examples of the reports that you expect and ensure that they can deliver the information needed in the required format. If possible, include sample reports in the RFP.

- *Vertical Expertise.* Look for vendors that have experience with your vertical market, unless you are willing to take complete responsibility for teaching the vendor your business or are building your own site.

- *Cost.* Calculate all costs for the next 2 years, if possible. Gather the cost of all activities from agent, supervisor, and managerial salaries (if the center handles them that way), telecom and technical support costs (if they are not bundled), training and coaching (if not bundled), QM, and so on.

- *Management and Supervisor Ratios.* Determine the ratios the center generally provides and find out if the center is willing to make any changes you need and what that might cost your organization.

- *References.* This is a step that companies too often skip, but it is essential to the success of your offshore implementation. Get five references, ideally from corporations with similar functions. Speak to the references and find out what the vendor does well and which areas need improvement. Be prepared to address any area of weakness in the contract.

- *Implementation.* The RFP should include many questions about the cutover and implementation. Look at the outsourcer's roll-out plan and be certain that it addresses your company's needs.

A comprehensive RFP is a great tool for collecting information, but it is also a means of communicating to vendors what your company expects from them. Good vendors will turn down business after reviewing RFPs that exceed their operational capabilities. Indicate to the vendors that their RFP responses will be attached to any eventual agreement. This prevents vendors from making claims they cannot keep.

As this is a time-consuming process, you should send the detailed RFP to only five vendors and select only three vendors for the site visit phase of the selection process.

Site Visit

A visit to the proposed site(s), regardless of location, is an essential component of the selection process. When you go to the site, be prepared to spend a full day observing contact center operations and interacting with agents.

Many offshore outsourcers are in new buildings and have up-to-date technology. Most of these vendors have formal programs to show prospects how they operate. It is important to sit through the standard presentations and site tour, but it is just as important to spend an entire day watching actual performance, listening to calls, and seeing how well the vendor functions. If the staff is rushing about and everyone looks confused, you can be sure the vendor is not appropriate for your organization.

Final Selection

Once you have analyzed the data—economic, socioeconomic, and RFP responses—and conducted site visits, select the top two candidates and negotiate the best deal for your company. It is always good to have at least two viable contenders so your company will have negotiating leverage.

Service Level Agreements

Service level agreements are the accepted method for defining service quality and operational parameters that outsourcing partners should deliver. Many outsourcers have standard SLAs; if your company does not have its own, go ahead and use what the vendor provides as a starting point. If your company has its own SLA, then include it in the RFP and insist that the vendor adhere to your SLA requirements. Most outsourcers will agree to adhere to a prospect's SLA, so if a vendor is not willing to meet your company's service needs, find one that will. (Outsourcers should make your job easier, not harder, and it is their responsibility to meet your requirements.) Service level agreements should address all areas of the relationship and not be limited to contact center productivity and quality measures. The SLA should address these categories:

1. *Operating Hours.* Days and hours of operation. Be sure to specify holidays and define service requirements for each of those days.
2. *Work Definition.* Define the work that agents must perform. This section should identify your company's specific inquiry categories, such as account retention, cancellations, loyalty clubs, general customer service, collections, technical support, games, billing, and so on. It should also specify the channels that the outsourcer would be required to support, such as phone, e-mail, chat, fax, and mail. If specialty handling is required, describe what is necessary. For example, if a company selling technical products concentrates on a demographic group that requires very patient handling and extra time, be sure to explain this in the work definition section. The purpose of including these requirements is to set expectations properly and avoid renegotiations too soon after a contract is signed.
3. *Processes and Procedures.* As long as it does not give away a competitive advantage, include your contact center operating policies and procedures in the RFP and ask the outsourcer to review them and determine if they can comply. If your company does not already have formal policies and procedures, draft a document outlining your approach to handling customers. This is a frequently overlooked step that can prevent much misunderstanding between outsourcers and their clients.
4. *Agent Quality.* Define agent quality guidelines for outstanding, good, average, and unacceptable performance—your company should set the

standards, and the outsourcer must agree to comply. Define a process for addressing agents who need improvement and rewarding those who are outstanding. You should also define what you want in a QM program, including the number of calls and e-mails to be reviewed per agent per week. Be sure to insist on doing both voice and screen quality management. If possible, include your QM evaluation form(s) in the RFP. The QM program must also allow you to monitor calls remotely, at your discretion.

5. *Agent Coaching.* Detail the coaching you expect for customer service agents. Define the frequency and approach—or ask the outsourcer to provide this information and make sure it complies with your company's method of handling agents. Coaching is important for keeping agent attrition rates low.

6. *Agent Training.* Specify the training necessary to prepare agents to handle your company's transactions. It is ideal to include a training program in the RFP. It is also necessary to define a minimum acceptable level for communication skills, accent, cultural knowledge, and other factors that are important to your customer base. If the agents' accents are so strong that your customers cannot understand them, then the fact that they cost 50 to 80 percent less will not help you because you will lose business.

7. *Escalation Procedures.* Set standard and exception escalation procedures. Define the types of transactions that should be escalated and the escalation time frames. It is important to establish open communication with your outsourcer and to invite the vendor to escalate back to your company when necessary. The purpose here is to avoid losing customers because the outsourcer's staff refused to let them speak directly to your company—a common problem in today's offshore outsourcing environment.

8. *Technology.* Define all technology requirements. It is highly recommended that you select an outsourcer that already has most systems installed. Definitions to address include the following:
   • The switch and how calls are handled, IP or TDM
   • Telecommunications—what service is required and what needs to be on a virtual private network (VPN)
   • Interactive voice response and speech recognition
   • Customer relationship management servicing suite
   • Customer servicing systems

- E-mail response management system
- Chat and collaboration capabilities
- Web self-service
- Knowledge management system
- Logging
- Quality management
- Surveying
- Workforce management
- Performance management
- Reporting
- Analytics

9. *Uptime and Performance.* The contact center outsourcer must commit to 99 percent uptime and provide monthly reports reflecting performance.

10. *Backup and Contingency Plans.* The contact center must have a plan to minimize business disruptions. The plan must comply with your company's backup and contingency standards.

11. *Reporting.* The outsourcer must report on a timely basis in pre-established formats. They should also include report formats in their RFP response to ensure that they provide the necessary information.

12. *Transaction (Call, E-Mail, Chat/Collaboration, and Mail) Reporting.* This is a standard SLA category that outsourcers address. It should reflect the following:

   - Call, e-mail, and chat/collaboration management reports, including, but not limited to:
     1. Volume of calls received and handled per half-hour, hour, day, week, and month.
     2. Volume of e-mails received and handled per half-hour, hour, day, week, and month.
     3. Volume of chat/collaboration sessions received and handled per half-hour, hour, day, week, and month.
     4. Volume of mail/faxes received and handled per half-hour, hour, day, week, and month.
     5. Call center service level performance measured per half-hour on a daily, weekly, and monthly basis.
     6. Agent productivity reports on a daily, weekly, and monthly basis. This report should be run for each agent, function, group, and the overall contact center. The report should include:

- Number of calls handled
- Average talk time
- Average after-call work time
- Average handle time
- Number of sales by category
- Total sales revenue
- Percent of sales opportunities closed
- Commission report by category

7. E-mail response time report: Time required to respond to customer e-mails, on a daily, weekly, and monthly basis for each agent, function, and group, and the contact center.

8. E-mail volume report: Total number of e-mails received by department, average time to send a customized response, average number of e-mails in each e-mail stream, average time to fully resolve customer e-mail inquiries, average time spent on each e-mail. Report should be for each agent, function, group, and the contact center.

- Percentage of calls resolved during the first contact
- Call and e-mail detailed reports reflecting the content of transactions, including:
  1. List of reasons people call
  2. List of recommendations to decrease the transaction volumes for calls and e-mail

Contract Terms and Conditions

Most outsourcers have standard terms and conditions (T&Cs) they would like their customers to adopt. But experienced negotiators generally prefer to provide their own T&Cs and then allow outsourcers to make changes. This gives control back to the buyer. It is recommended that you include T&Cs in the RFP and ask vendors to comment on anything they would like to change. This will streamline the contract negotiation phase of the effort.

Contract terms and conditions are the jurisdiction of lawyers, but here are some recommended guidelines:

1. Use your own contract.
2. Length of agreement: Do not sign up for more than one year. Out-

sourcers will want to tie you into long-term agreements. Do not do it, particularly not the first time you are doing business with a vendor. Yes, it would be expensive to move servicing to another outsourcer or back to its original location, but it would be more expensive not to—in terms of lost customers—if the outsourcer provides poor service.

3. Cancellation clauses: Include clauses that allow you to break the contract if the vendor's performance does not adhere to your SLA requirements. Of course, there must first be procedures for addressing problems, but when these fail, you must be able to get out of the contract if the vendor continues to fall below the contracted level of service.

4. Incentives and penalties: Formalize both incentives for outstanding performance and penalties for poor performance.

5. Finalized SLA: Negotiating the SLA can take a long time, but it is an essential component of the contract. The vendor will want to sign the agreement and then address the SLA. Do not do it. Once the agreement is signed, you lose your ability to negotiate an effective SLA, which is critical to the success of your outsourcing effort.

6. Change-in-business clause: Include a clause that allows you to renegotiate your deal if your company undergoes a major change, such as a merger or acquisition.

Managing the Relationship

As challenging as it is to manage an outsourcer when the vendor is geographically close to your business, it is a great deal more difficult when the vendor is thousands of miles away. Distance is a factor that you must consider when deciding to offshore. Here are guidelines for successfully managing your relationship with an offshore outsourcer:

1. Manage the relationship as you would any outsourced activity, regardless of the geographical distance.

2. Locate a manager on site, particularly early in the relationship while the "kinks" are being worked out.

3. Visit the site frequently, at least once per month. (The outsourcer will tell you this is not necessary and, after time, it may not be.)

4. Assign a United States–based manager to oversee the relationship.

5. Speak to your outsourcer daily—avoid the "out of sight, out of mind" syndrome that often plagues outsourced activities.

6. Build formal and informal escalation policies; encourage the outsourcer to escalate inquiries with reward incentives. Set up a formal daily review session, particularly early in the relationship, and encourage the development of informal channels.

7. Randomly monitor customer inquiries and evaluate call and e-mail quality.

8. Conduct a baseline survey to determine customer satisfaction levels before outsourcing your contact center activities.

9. Conduct customer satisfaction surveys as frequently as your budget allows, but not less than quarterly after outsourcing your contact center, to ensure that customer perception of service quality is not slipping.

Offshore Outsourcing Best Practices

While offshore outsourcing is relatively new for contact centers, best practices are already available. Here are eight best practices that will improve your chances for outsourcing success:

1. Perform due diligence on prospective outsourcers, including investigating viability, financial review, technology assessment, customer references, site visits, discussions with managers and agents, and review of U.S. State Department country briefings and alerts.

2. Outsource only those functions where costs and requirements are well defined.

3. Do not rush into a relationship. Finalize the contract before beginning operations. This includes the following steps:
   - Establishing SLAs with rewards for outstanding performance and penalties for poor performance
   - Defining daily, weekly, and monthly reporting requirements
   - Developing a problem resolution process with teams of participants from the enterprise and the outsourcer
   - Defining minimum agent skill set, training, and performance criteria
   - Creating a process for increasing and decreasing costs in response to volume increases and decreases
   - Instituting a cancellation provision

4. Make sure the outsourcer has a formal QM program that includes:
   - Simultaneous voice and data capture
   - E-mail QM capabilities

- Remote monitoring
- Agent coaching program
- Joint QM evaluations conducted by the enterprise and the outsourcer
- Semi-annual agent reviews

5. Verify that the outsourcer has excellent training capabilities, including:
   - A formal training program and materials (if these are not already in place, develop them jointly)
   - Outstanding trainers
   - In-house staff capable of training on products, systems, communications, problem resolution, technical support, and e-mail
6. Identify internal resources to manage the outsource relationship on an ongoing basis.
7. Monitor the outsourcer closely, especially early in the relationship:
   - Visit site monthly to stay on top of performance.
   - Be sure site has videoconference facility to minimize nonessential travel.
8. Check all possible references before selecting a vendor. There are likely to be issues with many vendors because they are relatively new. It is important to know what the challenges are before entering an agreement.

Offshore Outsourcing Market

The offshore outsourcing market is large and growing. Here is a partial list of offshore outsourcing vendors by country. Many of the outsourcers listed have sites in different countries around the world.

Argentina: Teleperformance and Technion Communications
Austria: Alldirekt Telemarketing, Call and Mail Telefonmarketing, and Call Now
Barbados: NCO Group
Belgium: Filad, Phonecom, and Up-Call
Canada: Alliance Call Centre Services, Client Logic Inc., Convergys, The Faneuil Group, Minacs Worldwide Inc., Nordia, NuComm International Inc., Omega Direct Responses Inc., Protocol Communications, Sitel Corp., Source One Communications Inc., Teleperformance, Telespectrum Canada, Teletech Canada, and Vox Data

China: Channelbeyond, Honglian 95, and China Railcom
Czech Republic: Contactel
Denmark: Tele Danmark
Estonia: Baltcom
Finland: Call Wave and Oy NovaCall Ab
France: Client Center Alliance and SR. Teleperformance
Germany: INFON Communication Center e.K.
Greece: Call Center Hellas and Phone Marketing AE
Hungary: TeleMedia Interactive Service L.L.C.
India: B2K Corp., Daksh (purchased by IBM in 2004), Infosys Technologies, SlashSupport, The Sutherland Group, vCustomer, WebHelp, Wipro Spectramind, and 24/7 Customer
Ireland: Intercall Management, Momentum, Onecall, and Performance Marketing
Italy: Alterego, Atesia, and Magicall
Lithuania: Lintel
Mexico: Hispanic Teleservices Corporation (HTC)
Netherlands: Interfoon Call Centers and SNT
Poland: Call Center Poland SA and Telecom Media Management Group
Puerto Rico: AT&T of Puerto Rico and Atento De Puerto Rico Inc.
Romania: Media Sat
Russia: Imageland and Vulcan
Slovakia: Hermes Direct Marketing
Sweden: Transcom
Switzerland: Digicall, MediaLine Interactive Solutions AG, Phone Marketing, and Piramedia
The Philippines: Ambergris Solutions, Callworx, Inc., Convergys, Etelecare International, Infonxx Philipppines, People Suport, SVI Connect, Inc., and Sykes Asia Inc.
United Kingdom: 2Touch, Call Centre Support, ComXo, Dataforce, Integrated Telemarketing Limited, Leadline, Sitel UK, and ukcallcentre
Ukraine: Utel Contact Center

Offshore Outsourcing Checklist

It's difficult to make the decision to outsource your contact center activities abroad. The consequences of offshoring are complex and far-reaching, profoundly affecting staff and customers. Enterprises should follow the steps in this checklist to address all critical factors before making a decision.

❑ Identify contact center(s) for outsourcing and do a baseline analysis of their costs.

❑ Conduct ROI analysis to ensure that the savings from outsourcing are worth the effort.

❑ Analyze economic and socioeconomic issues and select country or countries.

❑ Identify unacceptable risk factors and eliminate problematic countries from the analysis.

❑ Identify all short- and long-term functional, operational, and technical requirements; draft RFP and issue it to five vendors.

❑ Analyze economic, socioeconomic, and RFP responses; select three vendors for site visits.

❑ Visit sites and select two vendors for final negotiations.

❑ Negotiate SLAs and draft contract.

❑ Clean up all operational and procedural challenges before migrating contact center activity to outsourcer.

❑ Migrate contact center activity to the outsourcer.

13

Creating a World-Class Real-Time Engaged Contact Center

The perception among consumers is that service quality has gone from bad to worse in recent years. Interestingly, the perceived decline coincides with the introduction of CRM, a business strategy supposedly dedicated to improving relationships with customers. Customer relationship management is a great concept and strategy whose implementation has fallen short in too many companies around the world. Customers don't want to be managed. They want to do business on their terms, using their channel of choice, when they want, and the way they want. The challenge is that enterprises must "manage" aspects of customer relationships in order to get the results they want: increased revenue and profitability. This inherent conflict between corporate goals and customer desires has presented great obstacles to early adopters of CRM projects.

Contact centers fulfill many essential roles for enterprises. They are the primary customer contact point for most companies. The contact center represents the voice of the customer to the enterprise and of the company to its customers. Contact centers touch more customers on a daily basis than any other part of the corporation. As a result, when customers think about a company, they generally recall their last experience with its contact center. The contact center's role has been underappreciated for years, although this is slowly changing, to the benefit of corporations and customers alike.

What Is World-Class Service?

It's challenging to provide world-class service, particularly because the standard changes frequently, as the bar for excellence continues to rise. Market perception is that service quality decreased in the early 2000s. Whether this is statistically accurate is irrelevant; customer perception is reality.

Enterprises are striving to keep pace with evolving customer expectations and are looking for ways to consistently please their customers. They are investing an increasing percentage of their budgets on customer-facing activities (sales, marketing, and service) and genuinely care about the quality of service their customers receive. Most companies would invest more money in their contact center if they knew that the result would be satisfied and loyal customers who are willing to spend more on their products and services.

The definition of world-class service is well understood, and most companies are striving to improve their service quality. World-class service organizations "wow" their customers by providing a consistently outstanding customer experience in all channels. This, in turn, requires a sophisticated and increasingly expensive technology infrastructure that "knows" customers' preferences and needs, and delivers exactly what each customer wants in the customer's channel of choice. In some cases, this means that service is provided proactively, even before the customer is aware that it's required. Consider, for example, a computer system that dials out for help as its performance deteriorates. It doesn't wait for a complete system failure, but proactively calls for service to avoid a system crash. In other cases, customers will be engaged. Consider, for example, the bank customer whose account is close to zero, with the imminent risk of bounced checks. The bank could reach the customer in his or her channel of choice—e-mail, phone, or pager—with an alert to make a deposit or access a credit line, before an overdraft occurs. All of these activities require real-time activities that will "wow" customers and create highly satisfied and loyal clients who will have no reason to look elsewhere.

Role of Senior Management in Providing World-Class Service

Companies that provide world-class and award-winning service do so because of the commitment of their senior management, which plays a pivotal role in service delivery by setting the budget, tone, and direction of the contact center. When contact centers are geographically separate from headquarters, not tied in with common and shared corporate goals and rarely visited by senior management, the message is that service is secondary. Alternatively, when contact center management is invited to participate in corporate goal setting, shares revenue goals with sales and marketing, and has open channels for communicating customer insights, the message is different, as will be the service. Only when senior management visibly supports the contact center will it be empowered to deliver service that differentiates it from its competitors.

World-class service requires senior management support, a collaborative operating environment, and an enterprise strategy that prioritizes customer satisfaction over cost reduction. From a systems perspective, it requires sophisticated and seamlessly integrated applications that share customer information with other departments on a timely basis in real time or near-real time. More than 90 percent of enterprises are one to two complete generations behind the leaders in providing outstanding service, but are eager to improve their performance. Less than 10 percent of organizations are perceived as contact center leaders and innovators, and an even smaller percentage is viewed as world-class contact centers—operating environments that consistently meet and exceed customer expectations for service excellence.

Best Practices for Building and Maintaining a World-Class Contact Center

It's difficult to build a world-class contact center, but it's even more challenging to maintain a competitive edge. As other companies catch up, what once was perceived as a world-class service eventually becomes the norm. The following is a list of best practices for maintaining a competitive service advantage and world-class status.

1. Senior management fully supports contact center initiatives.
2. Sales, marketing, and service share common goals.
3. Contact centers should be profit centers.
4. A steering committee from sales, marketing, and operational stakeholders reviews service quality on a monthly basis.
5. The organization has a collaborative operating environment that invites input from the contact center and prioritizes resolution of customer issues on a timely basis.
6. Contact center management has title equivalency with peers in sales and marketing.

7. Contact center service quality is benchmarked on a semi-annual basis to other world-class operating environments in a variety of industries.
8. The company has a culture that rewards high-quality service and considers it essential for revenue generation.
9. The systems environment is integrated and facilitates the sharing of customer information on a timely basis.
10. Customer satisfaction with the contact center is surveyed on an ongoing basis.
11. Customer insights are captured and responded to in real or near-real time.
12. Agents are invited to share customer insights and interact with colleagues in sales, marketing, and senior management in a collaborative operating environment.
13. All contact center operations, practices, policies, and systems are comprehensively reviewed every 12 to 24 months.

Building a Culture of Constant Change

World-class contact centers are based and managed on the philosophy of constant change. This is a large management challenge, as most people, including contact center staff, are more comfortable in a stable operating environment. The best contact centers in the world are unique in both subtle and obvious ways. The differences begin with the type of people hired and how they are trained, motivated, rewarded, and promoted. Although technology absolutely differentiates service offerings, it's the staff that leaves the lasting impression on customers and is the primary focus of surveys and customer satisfaction evaluations.

Building and maintaining a world-class contact center is an ongoing journey whose only given is change. It's tough to build a contact center with lasting and profitable customer relationships while constantly decreasing servicing costs. It's even harder to transition an existing contact center from good to world class, as it requires changes in every aspect of a contact center's culture, systems, process, and people.

To succeed in today's increasingly demanding and competitive environment companies must transform their contact centers into real-time engaged profit-oriented organizations that are as dedicated to providing world-class service as they are to meeting corporate goals. They must position themselves to take advantage of every customer-initiated contact. Figure 13.1 reviews the strategy, management, and technology issues

(*text continues on page 196*)

Figure 13.1: Steps for Building a World-Class Engaged Real-Time Contact Center

Contact Center Evolution	Strategy	Management	Technology
From call center to cost-oriented contact center	• Standardize service quality in all channels. • Create single point of contact for sales and service support. • Optimize use of self-service channels—web and IVR/speech recognition—to reduce operating expenses. • Focus on cost containment.	• Cost center. • Emphasize first-call resolution to improve customer satisfaction. • Focus on customer satisfaction and retention. • Hire and/or retrain agents to be "universal" and handle multiple functions.	• Hybrid TDM/IP-based, multichannel contact center infrastructure • Use universal queue. • Implement e-service functionality to reduce volume of calls to live agents. • Use QM to improve call quality and customer satisfaction. • Use KM to standardize and improve service quality.
From cost-oriented contact center to profit-oriented contact center	• Maximize revenue from every customer-initiated transaction. • Collaborate with sales and marketing to achieve revenue goals and improve relationships with customers.	• Profit center. • Shift contact center to a combined sales and service culture. • Share information with sales and marketing to increase revenue. • Up-sell and cross-sell with personalized offerings. • Leverage contact center data for lead generation and revenue. • Hire/train contact center managers who are politically adept and good with sales, marketing, service, IT, and financial analysis.	• Integrate stand-alone contact center servicing system with sales and marketing applications to share customer information. Use a CRM suite or build in-house. • Integrate contact center with enterprise front and back office systems, including ERP and supply chain, to facilitate data sharing, lead generation, and sales fulfillment. • Use up-sell and cross-sell applications.

From profit-oriented contact center to real-time engaged contact center		
• Open contact centers systems to share customer information with corporation on timely basis. • Emphasize real-time activities. • Establish shared corporate goals for customer revenue, satisfaction, loyalty, and customer lifetime value for contact center, sales, and marketing. • Use an analytical approach to sales and service that adapts to customers' needs and facilitates real-time support in each customer's channel of choice.	• Modify contact center supporting systems and processes to facilitate a real-time approach to sales and service. • Build a data warehouse or data mart that gives the contact center a holistic view of customers and facilitates segmentation based on projected customer lifetime value. • Analyze customer information and engage customers proactively through the entire customer life cycle. • Invite customers to use their channel of choice, but incent them to use the less expensive alternatives. • Empower agents.	• Log 100 percent of customer transactions. • Implement performance management to align contact center and corporate goals. • Use surveying software to receive direct input from customers. • Use XML and web services to open contact center to rest of company. • Implement real-time analytics applications to capture, analyze, and take action based on customer needs and insights. • Capture and structure customer communications and mine them for new revenue and service opportunities. • Implement flexible and mobile service that is cost effective yet convenient for customers.

enterprises must address to migrate their sales and service department to a world-class real-time engaged contact center.

Road Map for Transforming Your Contact Center into a Strategic Player

Providing world-class service is the goal of every contact center manager. This can best be achieved by building a real-time engaged contact center. The majority of enterprises today operate a hybrid contact center that meets some of the characteristics from each of the three categories in Figure 13.1. Most contact centers handle both phone calls and e-mails, but few have seamlessly integrated the two channels or standardized service quality. For example, few contact centers would consider giving up their phone-based QM program, but most have not yet consistently applied QM to their outgoing e-mails. Although most contact centers today are involved in revenue generation, whether through new customer acquisition, account retention, lead generation, or up-sell and cross-sell, few are profit centers that share goals with sales and marketing. Most contact centers, while professing a commitment to customer satisfaction and retention, still prioritize productivity above all. There is inherent conflict between enterprise objectives and contact center goals in too many companies today, resulting in poor service and customer perception. This will continue, to the dismay of contact center managers, agents, and customers, until senior executives view contact centers as strategic players essential to their company's success.

Migrating from a Call Center to a Cost-Oriented Contact Center

More than 85 percent of contact centers display some of the characteristics of the cost-oriented model. The majority of their processes remain consistent with phone-oriented call centers. They prioritize expense control and productivity above all other goals, including quality and customer satisfaction. Their migration to a contact center generally begins when they start to handle e-mails in addition to phone calls.

Core Strategies of Cost-Oriented Centers

As these centers begin to apply best practices for handling an increasing volume of e-mail transactions, they begin their formal transformation from call centers to cost-oriented contact centers. Cost-oriented contact centers concentrate on four strategies:

1. Standardizing service quality across all channels: Customers should be given flexibility to use whichever channel is most convenient at any given time and should expect to receive the same outstanding service in all channels.
2. Providing a single point of contact for sales and service: Customers do not want to call different contact centers to place an order and to ask for assistance. They want to place one call or send one e-mail that will take care of all of their business.
3. Optimizing the use of self-service channels, such as web and IVR/speech recognition, to reduce staff-related operating expenses: The idea is to use web-based self-service, touch-tone, and speech-enabled IVR to automate inquiries, transactions, and tasks that do not require the added value that can be provided by live agents. Freeing agents from handling repetitive and mundane inquiries allows them to focus on higher-value transactions, reduces operating expenses, and improves agent retention.
4. Practicing cost containment: Reducing operating expenses and improving contact center productivity remains an essential goal.

Key Management Practices

The most influential and defining management practices applied in cost-oriented contact centers are the following:

1. *Managing Contact Centers as Cost Centers.* These centers are still viewed as an expense for their organization and, while important, are not yet fully appreciated by senior management. The cost center orientation affects the operation and purpose of these centers. They may collect leads or attempt up-sell and cross-sell, but they are primarily dedicated to providing good service at the lowest possible cost.
2. *Emphasis on First-Call Resolution to Improve Customer Satisfaction.* Customers expect their inquiry or transaction to be addressed during their

first call. World-class organizations will satisfy this requirement between 60 and 90 percent of the time, depending on the type of contact center.

3. *Focus on Customer Satisfaction and Retention.* This is the beginning of a shift from a pure productivity orientation, where calls per hour and average talk time were the priorities, to an emphasis on quality and customer satisfaction. However, as these are still cost centers, their drive for quality is as much a part of an effort to improve productivity as it is to satisfy customers.

4. *A Move Toward the Use of Universal Agents.* Universal agents are flexible people who can handle phone calls and e-mails, which require very different skill sets. Handling calls requires effective verbal communication skills; handling e-mails, the ability to write well. Another characteristic of universal agents is the ability to address service inquiries and to sell.

Essential Technology and Application Enhancements

Enhancing a call center and converting it to a contact center requires the addition of applications and technologies to support diverse constituencies (customers, prospects, partners, investors, and employees) and multiple channels (phone, e-mail, chat, fax), including:

1. *Hybrid TDM/IP-Based, Multichannel Contact Center Infrastructure that Includes a Universal Queue to Treat All Transactions Equally.*

2. *Use of a Formal QM System to Improve Call Quality and Customer Satisfaction.* Many call centers use some form of QM, but once a contact center is mature, a formal QM program becomes a requirement. When QM is applied properly and consistently it improves the quality of responses to calls and e-mails, which enhances customer satisfaction while increasing productivity. When agents are comfortable with what they have to do, they generally do it more quickly and more accurately, resulting in productivity improvements and reduction in customer callbacks.

3. *Use of KM Applications to Standardize and Improve Call Quality.* Not all contact centers require KM, but it's essential for those that provide technical support or handle complex products.

Migrating from a Cost-Oriented to a Profit-Oriented Contact Center

It's essential that contact centers continuously evolve to keep up with dynamic and demanding customer expectations. A phone-oriented call center may very well have provided world-class service 3 years ago, but if its phone agents are not able to identify and respond to issues raised in customer e-mails, it is not outstanding today. Contact centers are at different stages of development and should strive to improve their performance on an ongoing basis. At no time should a contact center sit back and be satisfied, as that is when it will lose its edge. If budgets are tight and technology investments are not possible, the contact center should concentrate on enhancing processes and procedures.

Enterprises that have successfully migrated from call centers to cost-oriented contact centers should begin the next stage of their evolution to profit-oriented contact centers. This is an even bigger step, as it requires the support of senior management, including the CFO. The CFO must approve the transition from a department that incurs costs and reduces the corporation's profitability to one that generates revenue. This has corporate implications because it changes how the contact center is viewed and, from a practical perspective, how it accounts for its revenue. It also affects the role of the contact center within the company. As of the end of 2003, less than 10 percent of contact centers were profit centers. By the end of 2010, more than 40 percent will be profit centers. This is the group from which world-class contact centers are identified, as they are the most innovative and best positioned to deliver differentiated service.

Key Strategies for Profit-Oriented Centers

Contact centers are being asked to contribute to the corporation's bottom line. To do so, they must focus on generating revenue in addition to their service responsibilities. Cost-oriented contact centers that are transforming to profit-oriented contact centers will concentrate on the following two strategies:

1. *Maximizing Revenue from Every Customer-Initiated Transaction.* Agents are motivated to look for new opportunities to increase revenue and customer

satisfaction every time a customer reaches out to the enterprise. Customers are much more receptive to offers when they initiate the contact than when they receive a telephone call, e-mail, or postal mail solicitation.

2. *Collaborating with Sales and Marketing to Achieve Revenue Goals and Improve Relationships with Customers.* Sales, marketing, and service have to put their differences aside and work together if they want to retain and build profitable customer relationships. The debate continues within corporations as to whether customers belong to sales, marketing, or customer service. The answer has always been that customers don't belong to a company or any one department. Customers choose to do business with companies that satisfy their needs. When sales, marketing, and service work together, the corporation's overall appreciation of customer needs increases, with each group adding its own unique insights. Unfortunately, due to historical and functional differences, the three primary customer-facing groups work together only when forced to by senior management. However, once they get underway and realize the benefits, cooperation grows, as do customer profitability, satisfaction, and loyalty.

Core Management Practices

Profit-oriented contact centers add a level of complexity to the management challenge. Openness and flexibility are required to integrate the contact center with the rest of the enterprise. The defining management characteristics of profit-oriented contact centers are:

1. *They are profit centers.* Converting a contact center from a cost center to a profit center is essential for the success of the operation. It sets the stage for the rest of the changes.
2. *They have a combined sales and service culture.* This is one of the more challenging management requirements, as it is difficult to change the culture of a department and retrain agents. To succeed, contact center management is going to need to change its training programs and reward and motivation systems to encourage agents to sell in addition to providing outstanding service.
3. *They share information with sales and marketing to increase revenue.* Processes are put in place to ensure that customer information is shared with decision makers on a timely basis. Contact centers become involved in the design of sales and marketing campaigns.

4. *They identify and use personalized up-sell and cross-sell to increase revenue and customer satisfaction.* Contact center agents are motivated and rewarded for improving and enhancing customer relationships. Identifying incremental revenue opportunities is as essential as satisfying each and every customer.

5. *They have contact center-specific goals for lead generation and incremental revenue.* In the past, contact centers were asked to generate revenue, but these objectives often conflicted with productivity goals. When agents asked customers about new opportunities, it added time to a call. In profit-oriented contact centers generating revenue is a priority and is measured at the agent, department, and overall contact center levels with performance management tools. Agents still need to be evaluated on productivity, but a more balanced scorecard also considers revenue generation, quality, and customer satisfaction.

6. *They are managed by politically adept leaders who are as knowledgeable about sales, marketing, IT, and finance as they are about service.* In order to gain the respect of peers, contact center leaders must be more open in reaching out to other departments. A common complaint about contact centers is that they are narrowly focused and do not understand the big picture. To address these concerns, contact centers should be led by individuals who are comfortable forming partnerships throughout the corporation. Once the perception of the contact center changes, the result will be increased cooperation, which makes corporate profitability goals easier to achieve.

Core Technology Enhancements

New technology must be implemented to support the strategy and management changes required to transition from a cost-oriented to a profit-oriented contact center. The changes are necessary to integrate contact center systems with sales, marketing, and the back office and to ensure that all customer requests and sales are fulfilled on a timely basis. System changes include:

1. *Integrating the stand-alone contact center servicing system with sales and marketing applications to share customer information.* This can be accomplished by using a CRM suite or building in-house. Facilitating the opening and sharing of customer information requires the integration of existing cus-

tomer service and support and/or telesales applications with customer systems in sales and marketing, or implement a CRM suite from vendors such as Amdocs, Chordiant Software Inc., Epiphany, Inc., KANA Inc., Onyx Software Corporation, Oracle, PeopleSoft, Inc. (acquired by Oracle in 2005), SAP, and Siebel Systems, Inc.

2. *Integrating contact center with enterprise front- and back-office systems, including ERP and supply chain, to facilitate data sharing, lead generation, and sales fulfillment.* The most effective contact centers are seamlessly integrated with enterprise systems so that they can satisfy customers and communicate with other operating areas on a timely basis.

3. *Using up-sell and cross-sell applications.* Profit-oriented contact centers require formal applications to support sales so that they can meet corporate revenue goals. The informal sales processes used in many cost-oriented contact centers must be replaced with systems designed to convert incoming inquiries into customized offerings and smaller sales into larger ones.

4. *Logging 100 percent of customer transactions.* There are many reasons to record 100 percent of calls. The FTC's DNC legislation requires most contact centers that sell to U.S. customers to log their calls. Logging can also protect companies from frivolous lawsuits. A more positive reason to log calls is to be able to mine them with speech analytics to identify customer trends, insights, and needs. Once identified, the data can be used to generate revenue and improve customer satisfaction.

5. *Implementing a performance management system to align contact center and corporate goals.* As contact centers evolve from cost-oriented operating environments to profit centers, in addition to capturing productivity metrics they need systems to measure their success in revenue generation.

6. *Using surveying software to receive direct input from customers.* For contact centers to respond in real time, they need to know what customers are thinking. Direct customer input is also essential for sales, marketing, and delivery organizations. In order to take a 360-degree view of a contact center's performance, enterprises need the timely feedback on products and service from customers that can only be obtained from surveys.

Migrating from a Profit-Oriented Contact Center to a Real-Time Engaged Contact Center

Changing the culture of a contact center from cost-oriented to a profit center that is measured against corporate revenue objectives instead of departmental productivity goals is challenging and will take time, new systems, and outstanding leadership that is supported by senior management. The next transition to a real-time engaged contact center will be even more difficult, but financially rewarding for companies that make the necessary investments in their staff, process, and technology.

Key Strategies for a Real-Time Engaged Center

Contact centers that are transitioning from profit-oriented contact centers to real-time engaged contact centers must implement the following strategies:

1. *Open contact center practices and systems to share customer information with the corporation on a timely basis.* One of the most common (and fair) complaints made about contact centers is that they are too closed. Sales and marketing organizations often find it difficult to obtain the information they want from contact centers about customers. The result is that these organizations are frequently at loggerheads and do not cooperate with each other. Assigning common and shared goals to sales, marketing, and service will help, but will not resolve the problems of providing external departments with relevant and timely customer information. This will happen only when contact centers convert to open and non-proprietary systems that can be accessed by other operating departments.

2. *Emphasize handling of more customer activities in real time.* Contact centers perform the majority of their activities in real time, with the exception of e-mails (which ideally should be handled within an hour of receipt). Contact centers have traditionally performed service in real time and other activities as follow-ups. For example, they often provide outstanding service, but instead of making and booking the sale at the point of contact, they simply capture leads. Contact centers should migrate most customer-based transactions, including sales, to real time to minimize

follow-up. This will cost more at the front end, in the contact center, but will reduce overall operating expenses.

3. *Establish shared corporate goals for customer revenue, satisfaction, loyalty, and customer lifetime value for the contact center, sales, and marketing.* For contact centers to be viewed as contributing corporate citizens, they must share goals with sales and marketing.

4. *Use an analytical approach to sales and service that adapts to customers' needs and facilitates real-time support in each customer's channel of choice.* Use analytics proactively to identify new opportunities for individuals and groups of customers. Be prepared to engage customers in their channel of choice when they are most open to new opportunities.

Key Management Practices

There are many advantages to engaging customers in their channel of choice at the point of contact. Building a profit-oriented real-time engaged contact center requires further modifications to management best practices. These changes will include:

1. *Modifying contact center supporting systems and processes to facilitate a real-time analytical approach to sales and service.* This is both a management and systems task. When contact centers modify their approach to handling customers, all of the management systems, such as workforce management, QM, e-learning, performance management, business intelligence, surveying, reporting, and real-time analytics, must be changed to support and encourage the new practices.

2. *Building a data warehouse or data mart that gives the contact center a holistic view of customers and facilitates segmentation based on projected customer lifetime value.* Contact centers need tools so that they can match service quality appropriately. For example, customers who are not profitable should be invited to use self-service systems. Customers who are profitable should be serviced in their channel of choice during every transaction. Of course, calculating a customer's lifetime value remains a challenge in most organizations. As a result, many companies look at a customer's current profitability, which can be a costly mistake. Consider the Harvard Law School student who may not yet be profitable but is likely to be very valuable in later years. If a company limits this individ-

ual to self-service systems when he is in school because he doesn't buy a lot of product, it's likely that he will change service providers as soon as his financial situation allows, which is exactly when he becomes more profitable. Contact centers depend on marketing to provide them with the data to stratify customers and are only as accurate as the information they receive.

3. *Analyzing customer information and feedback and engaging customers proactively through the entire customer life cycle.* There is no question that the best time to engage customers is when they reach out to your organization. When they do, you must be prepared to address their current and anticipated needs by continuously analyzing their buying and servicing patterns. If analysis indicates that a customer is going to call on the fifth of every month for a balance inquiry, it is cost effective and better service to have an IVR call out to that customer with that information. The proactive activity that results from analysis of customer servicing patterns is likely to create a loyal customer who is delighted with your service. You will have achieved the goal of providing world-class service while decreasing your servicing costs by moving the call from a live agent to an IVR.

4. *Inviting customers to use their channel of choice, but giving them incentive to use the less expensive alternatives.* Customers do not want to be told how to do business with a company; they want the flexibility of using the channels that are most convenient for them at any given time. For example, a customer may prefer using chat for inquiries, an increasing trend, but will use the phone when in the car. As chat is generally a less expensive channel to support, customers can be motivated to use this or any other self-service channel by giving them a small savings on their next invoice if they do not call. It is critical to reward behavior that benefits your company but not to penalize customers for engaging in their preferred behavior.

5. *Empowering agents.* This is critical for the success of your real-time engaged contact center. Contact center agents are being asked to make tough decisions in increasingly complex operating environments. Train agents and give them parameters, but invite them to become advocates by empowering them to make the right decisions for your company and its customers. Keep in mind that happy and satisfied agents communicate their feelings to your customers and can profoundly affect customer satisfaction.

Core Technology Enhancements

To construct a real-time engaged contact center that provides world-class service, new business strategy and management practices must be supported by system changes. The system changes include:

1. *Using XML and web services to further open the contact center to the rest of your company.* All new contact center systems should use XML for data integration and exchange, and web services to facilitate integration. The goal is to open all contact center systems so that customer information can be accessed and used by all stakeholders on a timely basis.

2. *Implementing real-time analytics applications to capture, analyze, and take action based on customer needs and insights.* The idea is to immediately use the information that customers freely share with contact centers, while the customer is still on the phone or in near-real time. To realize the greatest return from real-time analytics applications, the results—what customers bought—must be fed back into the enterprise data warehouse and analyzed for additional insights and opportunities. This process results in a closed-loop real-time analytics framework.

3. *Capturing and structuring customer communications and mining them for new revenue and service opportunities.* Generating new revenue and customer and asset retention are key to the success of any enterprise and are critical functions supported by contact centers. In addition to needing customer information for use in real time, many sales and marketing organizations are reaching out to contact centers and asking them to share customer insights that can be used to generate better and more profitable campaigns and sales programs.

4. *Implementing flexible and mobile service that is cost effective yet convenient for customers.* It's essential to enhance the analytical tools and capabilities of contact center agents to improve the bottom line. But contact centers must never lose sight of their primary objective of providing convenient and cost-effective service. Real-time engaged contact centers should be IP-enabled and should use session initiation protocol (SIP) to facilitate the handling of different devices.

Each of the three contact center categories builds upon the infrastructure that preceded it. A complete list of required technologies for the real-time engaged contact center can be found in Chapter 3 on contact center infrastructure.

World-Class Contact Center Checklist

It's important to strive to provide world-class service and to address individual aspects of great service, even if your contact center does not satisfy every requirement. Few companies achieve world-class status the first time or even the second time they try. Most companies dedicate years to building the infrastructure and support staff to provide differentiated service. This checklist will help your company identify where it sits on the continuum.

Yes No

☐ ☐ Is your contact center a profit center?

☐ ☐ Does your senior management take an active interest in your contact center?

☐ ☐ Does your contact center share revenue goals with sales and marketing?

☐ ☐ Have you won any industry awards for outstanding service, such as the DALBAR in the insurance industry?

☐ ☐ Do you support multiple communications channels, including phone, e-mail, chat, fax, and mail?

☐ ☐ Are all of your communications channels seamlessly integrated so that a customer e-mail can be seen and addressed by phone-based agents?

☐ ☐ Are your agents empowered to make independent decisions within defined financial and process parameters?

☐ ☐ Do you have feature-rich and compelling web and IVR/speech recognition self-service environments so customers who want to help themselves can do so?

☐ ☐ Have you conducted a contact center benchmark study in the past 6 months?

☐ ☐ Do you survey your customers on a monthly basis and share this information with all stakeholders?

☐ ☐ Do you use real-time analytics applications to identify and mine customer opportunities?

If you answered Yes to every question, your contact center is positioned to be a world-class operation. If you answered No to some or most of the questions, your contact center needs work. Use the checklist to prioritize action items.

14

Maximizing the Benefits of the Real-Time Contact Center

I f you have a contact center, it's already a real-time operating environment. Most companies, from the smallest to the largest, have at least
one contact center, and many enterprises have several in their organizations. Some, such as customer service or sales departments, were established with the intention of servicing customers from a centralized organization. Others, like the HR department, never intended to have
contact centers but were forced into it by the large volume of phone and
e-mail inquiries received from employees. Some contact centers are formal and use many of the systems discussed throughout this book; others
are informal, utilizing just phones and ad hoc procedures developed over
time. Regardless of the intent or initial purpose, an increasing percentage
of the business population uses contact centers to deliver sales and service.
This presents tremendous opportunities (as well as great challenges) for
companies that make investments to allow them to leverage each and every
customer contact at the point of contact.

The question is how to leverage your existing contact center(s) to grow
revenue and provide an outstanding customer experience that builds
loyalty. It's taken the market 30 years to build the contact centers we
now have. They are not going to undergo a metamorphosis overnight or
even within a few months, as they are inherently complex operating environments. Paradoxically, the easier components of the transition will be
changing the people, process, and technology—no small task. The harder
part will be changing senior management's mindset about the role and
value of contact centers.

Real-Time Contact Centers:
Revenue Generators and Competitive Necessity

It's not going to be easy to migrate reactive service infrastructures to real-time proactive engaged and profit-oriented operating environments, but enterprises *have no choice*. Companies that want to differentiate themselves and reduce the cost of sales and service—requirements in today's world of commoditized products and services—*must* migrate to real-time contact centers. Enterprises require real-time contact centers that are as dedicated to increasing their company's bottom line as they are to satisfying customers. It's not all about revenue generation, although it is about profitability. Enterprises that try to take shortcuts with service learn the hard way that service quality has a major impact on revenue generation. Companies that have not paid adequate attention to the relationship between service quality and revenue will be forced to accept this direct correlation.

Enterprises change slowly, as do their contact centers. But the evolution to real-time contact centers has already begun. Senior management and contact centers are slowly making the changes required to build more responsive and competitive corporations. Today, more than 90 percent of call and contact centers are still cost centers, dedicated to improving productivity and reducing expenses—which makes sense, as most are highly people-intensive. Presently, more than half of all contact centers are engaged in up-sell, cross-sell, or lead generation. This is an important step in realizing the revenue-generating potential of contact centers. As contact centers gain experience in selling and benefit from the increased cooperation and support of sales and marketing departments, they are becoming more respected within enterprises. By 2010, more than 40 percent of contact centers are expected to be profit centers, contributing significantly to their company's bottom line.

Technology:
An Essential Enabler of Real-Time Contact Centers

A company can provide outstanding service and sales support to a few customers without systems, but as the customer base grows, so does a company's need for technology to ensure that clients receive outstanding service. Contact centers can be basic and operate with just an ACD for queuing and routing customer transactions, or they can encompass a complex mix of systems and applications for managing customer interactions. Technologically sophisticated contact centers invest millions of dollars in core infrastructure, management systems, supporting systems, and enabling technologies to build effective, productive, and high-quality operating environments.

All contact centers are not created equal and therefore have different technology needs. Some contact centers do outdialing and therefore require a power dialer. Others support a technical help desk and require KM. Technology needs will be driven by the size and purpose of a contact center, as well as by the maturity of the department.

Contact centers committed to real-time service require new applications, such as real-time analytics, to identify new revenue opportunities at the point of contact or very close to the customer-initiated interaction. Real-time contact centers are typically dependent upon self-service technologies, such as IVR, speech technologies, and web self-service to automate routine transactions and free agents to spend time with customers who require live assistance. Building effective self-service environments is challenging, but the benefits far exceed the risks for well-managed implementations.

Contact Center Investments:
The Return on Investment and Total Cost of Ownership

The majority of contact center investments should pay for themselves within a year, although a few of the larger systems, such as contact center switches/infrastructure or a CRM suite, may take as long as 18 to 24 months before seeing a payback. There are a lot of technologies available that can be used in a contact center, but only the ones that make a positive contribution to the operating environment within a relatively short amount of time are worth an investment.

Before investing, a company should conduct an ROI analysis to carefully compare options, including whether to purchase, use an ASP, or outsource a function or system. In general, you should invest in a new application or system only if the investment meets your company's financial requirements for payback and financial return. There are times when your company may choose to invest in a new technology where the tangible ROI does not meet your financial thresholds. Not all benefits are easily quantifiable; sometimes "soft" benefits are the ones that give a company a competitive advantage.

Companies should also consider the TCO of technology investments. As the quality of hosted or on-demand solutions has improved radically during the past few years, renting or leasing an application can be a very good way to make a new system investment without a large up-front cash layout or the need to maintain the application. Having someone else maintain an application, as is the case in a hosted environment, can significantly reduce the TCO of a system investment. Of course, companies should conduct an ROI analysis to determine the most financially beneficial approach for acquiring new technology.

Do It Yourself, Hire Consultants, or Outsource?

There are many resources available for contact centers today. Companies can build and manage contact centers themselves, use consultants to assist with a portion of the project, or outsource the entire function to a domestic or offshore outsourcer. Offshore outsourcing became hot in 2003 and 2004, because it presented companies with the possibility of reducing servicing costs by as much as 50 to 60 percent.

There are few single initiatives that can yield such a significant level of savings, but the risks are also high. In 2004, the market saw a number of high-profile offshore outsourcing failures, including Dell and Lehman Brothers. Both companies brought back support functions from India because of customer dissatisfaction with service. And the State of Indiana, for example, realized that it wasn't politically savvy to offshore activities when the result was the displacement of American jobs. But these failures do not offset the hundreds of successes that do not hit the press. Offshore outsourcing is neither the great evil being depicted by the U.S. press and politicians nor a panacea for a troubled business. It is merely a business option for companies concerned about reducing costs.

Building a Real-Time Contact Center

While contact centers are real-time entities, shifting the mindset of management and staff requires major changes in people, process, and technology. Contact centers have to shift from reactive to proactive and engaged environments, from cost-oriented to revenue-generating organizations, and from a focus on managing productivity to building customer satisfaction and loyalty. To improve your chances for a successful transition, changes must take place over a period of time. World-class contact centers are always looking for ways to improve their performance, but they phase in new initiatives and systems so that innovations will be better received by both agents and customers.

World-class contact centers use technology as enablers, but it's the quality of their sales, service, or support staff that customers remember. When making investments in new technology, always build in time for staff training; contact centers operate in real time, but they require new processes, training, and systems to provide consistently outstanding, proactive, and engaged service.

A Final Word

This book is your guide for creating a world-class real-time contact center. Addressing the real-time opportunities for improving corporate profitability adds complexity to what is already one of the most technically and procedurally sophisticated departments within your company. It's not going to be easy to evolve your contact center from reactive and cost oriented to proactive and revenue generating, but the benefits and competitive advantage will be huge when you achieve this goal.

Building a world-class contact center has always been a multiyear, multiphase journey that begins anew when the original goals are met. The only way to maintain a competitive advantage is to continuously differentiate your company's performance from that of peer organizations. Transitioning to a real-time mindset requires the support of senior management, sales, and marketing in addition to changes in contact center systems, processes, and staff. Like most companies, yours has probably already invested in either a formal or an informal contact center. Why not make the most of the resources you already have by empowering your contact center to deliver outstanding service and be profitable?

Glossary of Abbreviations and Acronyms

Abbreviation or Acronym	Definition
ACD	Automatic call distributor
AHT	Average handle time
AICC	Aviation industry computer-based training committee
API	Application programming interface
ASA	Average speed of answer
ASP	Application service provider
BI	Business intelligence
CBT	Computer-based training
CFO	Chief financial officer
CIA	Central Intelligence Agency
CMS	Campaign management software
CRM	Customer relationship management
CSR	Customer service representative
CSS	Customer service and support
CTI	Computer telephony integration
DNC	Do Not Call
DS	Decision support
DTMF	Digital tone multifrequency
ERMS	E-mail response management system
ERP	Enterprise resource planning
FAQ	Frequently asked questions
FTC	Federal Trade Commission
FTE	Full-time equivalent
HIPAA	Health Insurance Portability and Accountability Act
HR	Human resources

IM	Instant messaging
IP	Internet protocol
IRR	Internal rate of return
ISP	Internet service provider
IVR	Interactive voice response
KM	Knowledge management
KPI	Key performance indicator
LMS	Learning management system
NLP	Natural language processing
NPV	Net present value
OLAP	Online analytical processing
PBX	Private business exchange
PC	Personal computer
PDA	Personal digital assistant
PSTN	Public switched telephone network
QA	Quality assurance
QM	Quality management
RFI	Request for information
RFP	Request for proposal
ROI	Return on investment
SALT	Speech application language tags
SCORM	Sharable courseware object reference model
SDK	Software development tool kit
SI	Systems integrator
SLA	Service level agreement
SMBs	Small and mid-size businesses
T&Cs	Terms and conditions
T&M	Time and materials
TCO	Total cost of ownership
TDM	Time division multiplexor
UQ	Universal queue
VoIP	Voice over Internet protocol
VPN	Virtual private network
VXML	Voice extensible markup language
W3C	World Wide Web consortium
WFM	Workforce management
WWW	World Wide Web
XML	Extensible markup language

Index